YOU ARE THE MONEY!

- REVISED EDITION -

YOU ARE THE MONEY!
- REVISED EDITION -

SELF-DEVELOPMENT
EQUALS
WEALTH DEVELOPMENT

WES HALL

FOREWORD BY
SIBYL MYERS, EDITOR

TOTALLY MOTIVATED PRESS
OMAHA, NEBRASKA

The Bible version used in this publication is
THE NEW KING JAMES VERSION.
Copyright © 1977, 1984, Thomas Nelson, Inc., Publishers.

Although the author and publisher have made every effort to ensure the accuracy and completeness of information contained in this book, we assume no responsibility for errors, inaccuracies, omissions or any inconsistency herein. Any slights of people, places or organizations are unintentional.

First Edition Printing 2000
Revised Edition Printing 2007

15 14 13 12 11 10 9 8 7 6 5 4 3 2 1

ISBN 0-9717055-0-X

Library of Congress Control Number: 2006909139

ATTENTION CORPORATIONS, UNIVERSITIES, COLLEGES, NOT-FOR-PROFIT AND PROFESSIONAL ORGANIZATIONS:

Quantity discounts are available on bulk purchases of this book for educational or gift purposes or as a premium for increasing magazine subscriptions and renewals. Special books or book excerpts also can be created to fit specific needs. For information, please contact the publisher, Totally Motivated Press, P.O. Box 11904, Omaha, NE 68111, or visit the Web site: www.totallymotivated.com

Edited by Sibyl Myers
Cover and book design by Carol Sayers,
Diversity Print & Graphics, LLC.
Printing Consultant Carol Corey, Corey Publishing

DEDICATION

This book is dedicated to those individuals who dare to find their purpose – and commit that purpose to the betterment of mankind.

"I believe this book can help anyone who is looking to better his or herself. Regardless of where you are in your life, we all have issues that we are trying to deal with. Let Wes guide you through ways to make your story a success story. The plan, the execution and the payoff are all right there inside of you. Remember, you are the money! Make it happen."

Iowa Rep. Wayne Ford (D-Des Moines) Co-Chair/Founder, Iowa Brown and Black Presidential Forum

ACKNOWLEDGEMENTS

You can't accomplish great things without great people, and I want to thank the great people who helped make this project a reality. I must first thank my Lord and Savior Jesus Christ for leading me to this message and allowing me to be the vessel through which it is delivered to the world.

I want to thank my editor Sibyl Myers for continually staying true to this mission even when I tested her patience. It's been a long hard walk, but I think we finally got it right. Thank you for your energy, foresight and friendship.

My mentor and friend Les Brown is now and always will be the motivational trailblazer. You taught me so much and have been such a large presence in my development as a speaker. I can never repay you for your teachings.

Cloves Campbell, co-publisher of the *Arizona Informant*, you are "The Man." Thank you for your words of inspiration and for believing in me. Honorable Wayne Ford, thank you for being that big brother I needed. Our stimulating conversations over the years have led to my edification and continual growth – much love!

Dr. Joel Martin, thank you for your insight and words of wisdom. Carol Corey, you have been an angel to this project. Thank you for your guidance and your nurturing spirit. Carol Sayers, I sat across from you and told you my thoughts about the cover, and you let God work through you and brought my vision to life. Thank you for sharing your gift.

FOREWORD

The power of connection. Wes Hall has that rare gift of connecting with people -- whether it's audiences listening to his keynote address or readers learning from his motivational tips in his newspaper column or his book. His magnetic appeal attracts a diverse following – entrepreneurs, corporate executives, educators, community leaders, employees and youth.

It's one thing for a speaker to present a mundane message to an audience who responds with polite applause. But it's quite an extraordinary feat for a master speaker to instantly connect with listeners who walk away with the message etched in their psyches. That's the power of Wes Hall and the mass appeal of *You Are The Money!* In working with Wes over the past six years, I've seen the evolution of his concept of *You Are The Money!* as it was developed, tweaked and polished to take to the national stage. I've seen the magnetism of his message connecting with audiences and even casual listeners.

_____

"I Am The Money!," proclaimed an unexpected voice booming from a waiter in the back of the near-empty room, amidst the clatter of dishes being cleared from the tables. The breakfast was over, the presentation was finished, and the audience had moved to the business exhibits. Only the wait staff remained busily at work.

Wes Hall *(the keynote breakfast speaker)* and I *(his publicist)* returned to the room to pick up materials before leaving town. An hour earlier, Wes delivered a high-impact speech in that conference room in St. Louis to a capacity audience of minority entrepreneurs and corporate executives. He was selected as the breakfast speaker to jump-start the audience at the Business Opportunity Fair – and that he did! As part of his presentation, he explained his concept of *You Are The Money!* and how self-development equals wealth development. The connection with the audience was immediate with the room coming alive early in the morning with chants of "I Am The Money!"

But who knew that long after the presentation, Wes' mantra would resonate with an unknown waiter who heard the chants while working. The power of that connection struck a chord with me. Wes' message of *You Are The Money!* was so dynamic that not only did the intended audience of minority entrepreneurs and corporate executives embrace it, but also a waiter who just happened to be working in the room and found inspiration in the lesson and a greater appreciation for his own self-value.

I first met Wes Hall in 2000 while on assignment as a columnist/correspondent for the *Omaha World-Herald*. He told me about an upcoming special event he was spearheading to start a community radio station in Omaha. The guest speaker was Les Brown, world-renowned speaker and best-selling author, who was Wes' mentor. I thought the event was newsworthy and wrote a feature article for the newspaper.

Later, knowing I had 25 years of experience as a journalist, Wes asked me to edit his first edition of *You Are The Money!*, published in 2001. As a result, I became interested in learning more about his motivational presentations, inspired by his lessons of self-development. That led me to create promotional materials for him, assist with bookings and edit his weekly newspaper column entitled "Totally Motivated."

With his energized message attracting more widespread appeal and national attention over the past five years, the time is right for Wes to take *You Are The Money!* to the next level with this revised edition. And once again I am editing his book.

I've watched Wes' message take wings and travel across the country from St. Louis to Phoenix to New York. People across the country chanting, "I Am The Money!" A catchy phrase, no doubt, but it may sound like just capitalistic hype. So what does it really mean? At the heart of the message is how you can be a better person. It's a way of life. In other words, *You Are The Money!* is about living up to your potential and increasing your self-value.

It's a big concept that encompasses many aspects. Wes promotes his message in workshops and training programs focusing on areas such as team-building, conflict resolution, branding and leadership development. Those areas are keys to success in the workplace and the business world. He also has written a curriculum for students to strengthen their communication skills. And, he has developed products, services and training modules that show how to attract wealth through self-improvement.

You Are The Money! is about boosting your self-esteem, defining your purpose and finding the winner in you. It's all about self-development. The rewards await you.

Sibyl Myers
Editor

PREFACE

"**Attracting**" wealth and abundance into your life, that's the secret to success. But millions of people attempt to gain riches in the exact opposite manner. By way of failed learning, the masses view money as an external entity, and therefore chase it (like a horse chasing a dangling carrot).

Successful people understand the amount of dollars they receive in life is predicated on their personal investment. In other words, successful people understand they get out of life what they themselves put into it.

Money affects every aspect of your life. It determines where you live, the type of neighborhood you grow up in, the school you go to and the quality of education you receive. In many ways, the presence of money, or the lack of it, molds the lenses through which you see the world.

Few will admit how much of an impact money has on life, but all realize its enormous presence. Money can mean the difference between receiving a parent's blessing on a future spouse or a flat rejection. One of the first questions friends and family ask when inquiring about your new love is, "What does he/she do for a living?"

In this world, money can determine whether you live or die. A well-financed life affords you the best medical care, the best doctors and advanced medical treatment. A life absent of money can land you in the community hospital, with limited services, and out the door as soon as possible.

The gap between the haves and have-nots continues to widen. The richest 1% own approximately 50% of America's wealth, while 98% of all Americans have little or no net worth. The obvious question is, "Why?"

Why do so many able-bodied men and women struggle to make ends meet? Why do millions of people in America – one of the wealthiest countries in the world – live from paycheck to paycheck? How does one work for 20 years and retire with a sum total that still places him below the poverty line?

Is there a special formula for obtaining wealth that only the wealthy are aware of and keep quiet from the masses? Or, is there a basic equation to attaining and maintaining wealth? The answer is the latter, and through this book you will discover why.

Although *You Are The Money!* speaks of wealth and the creation thereof, it is much more that. It is a tool designed to bring out the best in you. It is a paradigm shift that will assist you in changing the way you see "you" as it relates to attracting abundance into your life.

If you currently are experiencing success in your field of endeavor, this book will encourage you to seek greater heights. It will challenge you to reach deeper inside yourself, discover your purpose and leave a lasting legacy.

If you are struggling to make ends meet and living a life of lack, this book will set you on course to self-discovery and provide greater insight to the workings of power that attracts wealth and abundance.

So prepare for a miraculous journey that concludes with you learning to be what God intended you to be – a free and powerful being. You are about to learn the art of "attraction." Let me show you why "You Are The Money!"

FROM THE AUTHOR

Throughout this book are references to *We Shall 217*. I created that moniker some years ago after reconnecting with the Rev. Martin Luther King's message of "We Shall Overcome."

Coincidentally, the letters in my name – *Wes Hall* – are synonymous with *We Shall*.

The numbers 217 represent my birth date. There are few instances in the Bible where an actual date is mentioned. One is in *Genesis 7:11*: "In the six hundredth year of Noah's life in the second month, the seventeenth day of the month, the same day were all the fountains of the great deep broken up, and the windows of heaven were opened."

That occurrence (the great flood of 40 days and 40 nights) ushered out the old and made way for the new.

Thus, *We Shall 217* represents my calling and purpose -- to help people overcome barriers that limit their potential so they can live a life of purpose and abundance.

*"There are those who look at things
the way they are, and ask why . . .
I dream of things that never were
and ask why not."*

**Robert F. Kennedy,
quoting George Bernard Shaw**

YOU ARE THE MONEY!
CONTENTS

STAGE 1 – AWARENESS: THE PARADIGM SHIFT

1 YOU ARE THE MONEY!

STAGE 2 – SELF-EMPOWERMENT: INCREASING YOUR SELF-VALUE

2   GET ACTUALIZED

STAGE 3 – TOTAL BELIEF: BECOMING ONE WITH YOUR DREAM

3   MASTERING THE ART OF KNOWING

STAGE 8 – KEEPING YOUR EYE ON THE PRIZE: ELIMINATE DISTRACTIONS

8 SINGLE-MINDEDNESS

STAGE 9 – BUILDING YOUR EMPIRE: BRICK BY BRICK

9 ACTION!

STAGE 10 – DOING WHAT OTHERS WON'T DO: HAVING WHAT OTHERS WON'T HAVE

10 NAME POWER!

STAGE 11 – THE FINISH LINE: JOB WELL DONE!

11 FREEDOM!

STAGE 12 – GIVING BACK – SERVING OTHERS: LEAVING A LEGACY

12   GETTING CONNECTED

– AFTERTHOUGHT –
PUTTING IT ALL TOGETHER

STAGE 1
AWARENESS

The Paradigm Shift

– STAGE ONE –

*The employer doesn't pay your wages –
he just controls the money.
The product pays the wage.*

We Shall 217

YOU ARE THE MONEY!

Self-Development Equals Wealth Development

Except for lottery winners, heirs or others who fall into wealth, individuals who successfully establish a financial empire do so through *internal* fortitude and a deep understanding of self.

Your ability to generate wealth begins with you. You must first realize "You Are The Money!" It is not the scraps of paper you chase that enable you to live the life you desire – it is the amount of work you perform on yourself that increases your value and thus increases your monetary return.

When you diligently work to increase your self-value, you become even more valuable to you and your employer. The company benefits from your efforts in many ways. For example, your personal success creates more positive energy in you. Others are directly or indirectly motivated by your self-improvement, and your additional knowledge also increases your capacity to help the company grow by your creation of new ideas, products or services. And if you really are a superstar, you may go on to

YOU ARE THE MONEY!

start your own business or create your own products and services. Your ability to obtain the wealth you desire requires a major paradigm shift. You have to take your sights off the money and refocus on your personal development. The logic is simple – if you want to make a million dollars, you must increase your worth to $2 million.

Tiger Woods, the amazingly talented golf superstar, is a glowing example of the "You Are The Money!" concept. Tiger was only two years old when his dad Earl Woods began teaching him golf. The two of them worked tirelessly on Tiger's form and understanding of the game.

Soon Tiger was performing at a rate beyond his years, and his skills attracted the attention of powerful people inside and outside the game of golf. His phenomenal talent generated a buzz, and major sponsors were following his every move.

By the time he made the announcement he was turning pro, Tiger had endorsement offers flooding in. The sports icon Nike beat all bids with a $100 million offer. The young sports prodigy became a multimillionaire before he played his first game as a professional.

Upon closer observation you will recognize it wasn't Tiger or Earl's pursuit of the money that generated their fortune – it was the tireless commitment to excellence that "attracted" millions. Tiger's near-perfect swing of the golf club, along with his powerful mental conditioning, is *the money*.

You Are The Product

Keep in mind, the employer doesn't pay your wages – he just controls the money. The product pays the wage. In other words, customers exchange money for the value of the product or services. A superior product or service "attracts" the money that pays the wage.

That premise is worth exploring. It is interesting to observe the way many individuals view their work process. The average person goes to work, puts in time on the job and expects to get paid for hours worked.

An employee sees his job as a way to make ends meet – something he does to keep a roof over his head. Closer observation will reveal the company is in fact paying each person, to some degree, for the amount of skills, talent or schooling he brings to the table (his or her personal self-investment).

The company places an ad in the paper to fill a position. Prior to that, the company determined how much the job was worth. The employer then sets out to find the person (product) who has invested time in himself to satisfy the needs of the position.

You probably have heard the term "over-qualified." That means the person applying for the job is worth more (has invested more in him or herself) than the job is worth or the employer is willing to pay.

The Product Pays The Wage

Let me provide you with a simple way to understand the "product" concept. The NBA is the employer; LeBron James is the product. The PGA is the employer; Tiger Woods is the product. Sony is the employer; Christina Aguilera is the product.

Whatever your line of work, you are the product. Your employer's return from the work you produce must be greater than the cost to him. An easy way to understand that principle is to relate it to selling goods. A merchant would not stay in business long if he sold his wares for the same price he bought them.

Your success is predicated on understanding that equation. To garner the wealth you desire, you must build your self-worth so your value is greater than your purchase price.

Increasing Your Value

The obvious question is, "How do I increase my value?" The answer is through an add-on process, which refers to your self-investment. Each self-improvement item added to your resume increases your value.

The best way to understand the add-on process is to look at the automobile industry. A car may sell for $10,000 with no accessories. But each "added" accessory increases the car's value and subsequently costs you more money for the same vehicle.

A professional speaker, for instance, may command $100 per speaking engagement based on his voice and ability to share information. That same speaker can command $10,000 to $20,000 per speaking engagement if he adds value-increasing items to his resume.

For example, when a speaker writes a book or develops a curriculum on his area of expertise, he increases his value. By adding "author" to his resume, he sends the message to potential clients that he is well versed in his area of expertise.

A speaker seeking to increase his value also may explore ways to gain publicity for his product or service. When you add newspaper articles, magazine features or TV coverage about your product or service to your promotional package, you increase in value, and the price of your personal stock goes up.

The same process holds true in many ways for other occupations. You can substitute TV coverage for certification if you are an aspiring teacher. If you desire to go from Sergeant to Deputy Chief of Police, obtaining a degree is a great way to start.

You can add to your personal value in many ways. Pursue options that best enhance your resume. For example, how many companies are looking for bilingual employees?

You can study at home, add value to yourself and be better armed to attract more money into your world. The more you do to improve yourself, the greater your personal value. The greater your personal value, the greater your monetary return.

The Law of Attraction

The attraction process is multifaceted, consisting of many variables. The main principle of attraction is power. Many people mistakenly equate the possession of money with the possession of power. That couldn't be further from the truth. Money is a byproduct of power.

You've heard the expression, "A fool and his money are soon parted." Others would say, "I don't know how they – a fool and money – got together in the first place." But they do, at times, find their way to one another, and their union does not equal power.

Your ability to gain power will come as a result of self-mastery. It does not matter which craft or discipline you choose to master. What matters is the degree of proficiency you acquire within your chosen discipline.

The more work you perform on yourself, the more attention you generate. Remember when Arnold Schwarzenegger was a body-builder (before he became governor of California)? Arnold came to America with virtually no money. But before long, he built his body to the point it attracted attention. Soon he began to win major competitions. His well-defined body attracted endorsements, television exposure, fame and millions of dollars.

Arnold is one of the greatest testaments to my "You Are The Money!" concept. When you put his accomplishments into perspective, you come away with a solid understanding of how the concept works.

Each of us has a body, but how many of us simply can take off our clothes and command national endorsements? Arnold was able to recognize the value of a well-sculpted body. That body made him millions of dollars. His self-investment paid great dividends and even landed him a billion-dollar wife.

Again, I implore you to see the obvious. Arnold easily could have sought a job and tried to climb the corporate ladder to satisfy his need for money. He could have chased money like millions of Americans do. Instead he invested in himself, created personal power (authentic power) and "attracted" wealth and abundance into his life.

Let The Money Chase You

Instead of spending your life chasing money, create mastery in your craft, and let the money chase you. Your ability to perfect that aspect of your approach to money will set you apart from your peers.

Certain individuals in every field are highly sought for their services. While others struggle, those individuals have a constant supply of business and money. They seem to possess some secret that attracts business even in down times.

Here is an example of how you let the money chase you. Bob is a carpenter who specializes in refinishing basements. He is known for his meticulous work and attention to detail. He views each project as a piece of art he is creating for his customer.

When Bob began his business 10 years ago, he had no clients. All he had were his tools and his word. By chance, a family friend bought a new home and needed his basement finished. Word reached Bob, and he asked if he could do the job. Bob even offered to do the work at a reduced rate.

The friend agreed to take a chance on Bob who went to work remodeling the basement. Amazingly, Bob transformed the dull basement into a modern-day work of art. The homeowner was thrilled and spread the word to his friends.

Bob's telephone began ringing off the hook with people wanting his services. The increased demand allowed him to charge more for his work. Before long, he had a waiting list and even had to turn away business.

Bob's attention to detail and perfection of his craft were in high demand. Before he couldn't make ends meet, but now he had plenty of business. He no longer had to chase the money – the money was chasing him.

Become The Bar

When Bill Gates created Microsoft, he not only raised the bar, he became it. The same can be said of billionaire stock guru Warren Buffet or media icon Oprah Winfrey. But many people don't set their goals high enough while seeking to become their best.

One reason is tunnel vision. Individuals primarily compete on a local level. That might be great if you're in New York, Los Angeles or Chicago – the top three markets in the United States. But the competition might be limited in smaller markets.

When you only prepare yourself according to your current competition, you may not be competing at the highest level. Although you may be No. 1 in your market, you may find your skills lacking when compared to the nation's best.

A part of your regimen must include travel. You cannot gain the competency you require by operating in a box. You have to expand your sights, and you can do that by experiencing firsthand the environment of the highest achievers.

If you are to reach the top, you must create a new level of greatness and become the bar itself. You must learn how to work yourself into a white-hot ball of desire. Your focus must be unmatched, and you must become one with the concept of competing at your highest level.

Rare is the individual who can accomplish such a feat, but the reward is well worth the sacrifice. You only live once, and this is no practice round – this is the real deal. So gather your strength and determination to compete on life's highest plateau. For it is through that fire you will find your way to riches and glory.

*"Every moment is another opportunity
to turn it all around."*

Vanilla Sky, the movie, 2001

– STAGE ONE –
WORTH REMEMBERING

- Tiger Woods was only two years old when his dad Earl Woods began teaching him the game of golf. The two of them worked tirelessly on Tiger's form and understanding of the game.

- Tiger's phenomenal skills generated a buzz, and soon major sponsors were following his every move.

- The employer doesn't pay your wages – he just controls the money. The product pays the wage.

- The NBA is the employer; LeBron James is the product.

- To garner the income you desire, you must build your self-worth to the point where your value is greater than your purchase price.

- The simple reality is if you want to earn a million dollars, your self-value must be $2 million.

STAGE 2
SELF-EMPOWERMENT

Increasing Your Self-Value

– STAGE TWO –

*The greatest success you can achieve
here on Earth is becoming
what you were meant to become.*

We Shall 217

GET ACTUALIZED

Beyond Motivation

The 1990s was the era of motivation. If you are to compete and succeed in the New Millennium, you must become actualized. Motivation is as far from actualization as hoping is from doing. The secret to ultimate power is self-mastery, and self-mastery is gained through actualization.

In the words of famed scientist Abraham Maslow, *"We may still often (if not always) expect that a new discontent will develop unless the individual is doing what he is fitted for. A musician must make music, an artist must paint, a poet must write, if he is to be ultimately at peace with himself. What a man can be, he must be. This need we may call self-actualization, which refers to man's desire for self-fulfillment, namely, to the tendency for him to become actualized in what he is potentially. This tendency might be phrased as the desire to become more and more what one is, to become everything that one is capable of becoming."*

Actualization occurs when your potential matures into performance. Every initial undertaking is rooted in potential. It is only through repetition, which produces measurable results, that you become one with your attempts. A presidential candidate, for instance, may win the Oval Office, but it may take most of his first term before he actually feels like "The President." After performing the duties of the president and having people treat him as such, he soon becomes one with the title, and thus actualizes.

Actualization evolves through repetition and reward. When you perform to your capacity and meet with consistent approval, you begin to believe in your talents. That belief continually developed will create an attitude of certainty, a requisite for actualization.

Many people never attain actualization because they cave in to challenges and obstacles. They capitulate when the going gets rough and easily give up their goals and dreams. Every person who obtained greatness did so by overcoming tremendous difficulties.

Only one road leads to actualization, and that road is called "exposure." You have to expose yourself to scrutiny if you are to grow. You have to fail if you are to succeed. But your failures will be different than most because you understand that through failure you really are learning how to win.

A comedian, for instance, may perform in many venues and try a variety of material before he discovers what works. He may bomb in Iowa and receive an ovation in D.C. By the time he does New York, he will be one with his routine and qualified to don the title "comedian."

Actualization and Wealth Creation

The wealth-building component in becoming actualized manifests through your ability to interact with others in a way that reflects strength and knowing. Powerful people love to do business with other powerful people.

The moment a power broker comes into the presence of an actualized being, the recognition is immediate. There is no hiding a wellspring of knowledge. Even in its most secretive aspect, its power is apparent.

Whatever you choose to be, do it to the point of actualization. If you choose to be an actor, act on every occasion you can, for no pay if necessary. Act on a street corner, in a church, wherever and whenever you can. Do so until the people around you begin introducing you as "an actor."

When you reach that level of penetration, you will begin to think and feel like an actor. That internal feeling will demand greater fulfillment and lead you to seek greater opportunities. The right opportunity will present itself, and the wealth you seek will follow.

Your constant and exhaustive pursuit of excellence will lead you to other empowered people. Those individuals are connected with people and projects that can benefit you. Your passport to wealth and power will come from reaching the pinnacle of your being – and that is actualization.

Believe It, and You Will See It!

Are you able to move forward to your goal even if you cannot see it in your present sight? Consider this: If you left home to travel to another city 500 miles away, upon leaving your driveway could you see your destination?

Unless you have superhuman powers, the answer is no. If your tires blew out along the way, would the city you're traveling to move? If the engine fell completely out of your car, would the city move? Not one inch. You merely would repair your car, continue on your route and reach your destination.

You may have to adjust your time frame, but your initial goal of traveling to another city would remain intact. And so it is with any goal you choose to pursue. The key is to view your goal as a *fixed object* like the city you were traveling to in the previous scenario. Set your mind that your goal already is a reality even though you cannot see it right now.

That is how you must view the goal you want to reach. Know for a fact if you keep moving toward your goal, one day it will come into view. You must cease waiting for the goal to come into sight before you do the necessary things to make it happen. Remember the saying, "Success happens when proper preparation meets opportunity."

Your ability to move toward your goals and objectives, absent of the need to see them in your current reality, will enable you to maximize your energy and reduce your anxiety. You will begin to understand the universal law that governs time and discover the many forces that go into bringing your dreams into reality.

As an actualized being, you learn to believe in your innate powers. You realize you are not some accident waiting for a coincidental occurrence to make you complete. You understand the fullness of your capacities and move to become one with your destiny.

Your level of consciousness quells fear and allows you to call upon your greatness within. You begin to interpret information at a purer level, and you trust your inner-radar. You become acutely aware of your value as you bring to this world the beauty of your purpose.

Expect to Win!

Life will give you, in part, what you expect to receive. Do you really think you will attract a million dollars into your life? Do you really expect to live a life of power, love and abundance? Do you really think you will win the game of life?

Most people are "expectation challenged." They say all the right things, but when they look deep within, they discover they don't believe their own hype. They speak in terms of what they would like to produce instead of what they will, without exception, *produce.*

A trademark action of an actualized being is "writing a check that your actions must cash." When you reach the point of actualization, you know beyond a shadow of doubt what your capabilities are. You understand the reality of the statement, "The future is birthed out of the moment."

By way of that understanding, you do "in the moment" the things that will blossom into your visualized future. You toil daily to complete each task that adds substance to the dream you hold in your heart. And when energy, action, tenacity and vision combine with time, your actualized efforts will meet with an unimaginable success.

"Obstacles are those frightful things you see when you take your eyes off your goal."

Henry Ford

– STAGE TWO –
WORTH REMEMBERING

- The 1990s was the era of motivation. If you are to compete and succeed in the New Millennium, you must become actualized.

- Actualization occurs when your potential matures into performance.

- It is only through repetition, which produces measurable results, that you become one with your attempts.

- Actualization evolves through repetition and reward.

- Many people never attain actualization because they cave in to challenges and obstacles.

- Only one road leads to actualization, and that road is called "exposure."

- You have to fail if you are to succeed.

- The moment a power broker comes into the presence of an actualized being, the recognition is immediate.

- If you choose to become an actor, act on every possible occasion – do so until people around you start introducing you as an "actor."

STAGE 3
TOTAL BELIEF

Becoming One With Your Dream

– STAGE THREE –

"That day dawns to which we are awake."
Henry David Thoreau

MASTERING THE ART OF KNOWING

Turning Goals Into Results

*"**Knowing:** To perceive with certainty,
to understand, not to be doubtful."*
Webster's Dictionary

Turning your personal value into its monetary equivalent requires a greater-than-ordinary effort. That feat cannot be mastered through timid approaches. You must be able to generate the necessary amount of energy that allows others to see you as a marketable product.

The road to success is lined with obstacles and challenges, and sometimes you can't visually see the finish line. You may reach a point where you begin to doubt yourself and your efforts. In those times you must "know" who you are and "know" you are more than capable of completing the task.

When you operate in a state of "knowing," you see through obstacles. You become one with your mission and even the most trying circumstances are no match for your inner-resolve. The conscious level of "knowing" is the final frontier for any power broker determined to reach new heights and snatch victory from the hands of defeat.

There's a story about 100 mountain climbers preparing to climb Mount Everest. A psychiatrist interviewed each climber and asked, "Do you think you will make it to the top?" Most answered, "I'll give it my best" or "I'm going to try my hardest."

Only three of the 100 said, "I will." You can imagine how many climbers made it to the mountain top. If you said three, you were right. Those three had the mindset that produces victory. I call it the "knowing mindset."

The Knowing Mindset

"For verily I say unto you, that whosoever shall say unto this mountain, be thou removed, and be thou cast into the sea; and shall not doubt in his heart, but shall believe that those things which he saith shall come to pass; he shall have whatsoever he saith."
St. Mark 11:23

Knowing is a divine state of consciousness. Knowing leaves no room for anything except action. If you are to reach your maximum potential, you must master the art of knowing.

What then is knowing, and how do you master it? Knowing is a deep internal belief that comes from experiencing something in a tangible manner. It is the feeling you get when you put in the work and have total belief in the outcome.

**When you do the work on the inside,
obstacles on the outside don't stand a chance.**

The best way to understand and obtain a knowing consciousness is to observe the preparation of a marathon runner. The runner knows how taxing a 26-mile marathon can be so he prepares by running 40 miles.

If you prepare for a 26-mile run by running 40 miles, you have no fear of the 26. Your preparation enables you to "know" you can and will complete the race. Your ability to operate in a state of knowing frees your energy and allows you to compete with power and confidence.

Seeing The Invisible/Doing The Impossible

It was no coincidence that millions of people flocked to see the 1977 blockbuster sci-fi movie *Star Wars*. George Lucas, writer/director/producer, tapped into a concept that went to the very soul of the viewer. The Jedi was an entity that used "The Force" and operated in a total state of *knowing*. The character Yoda warned of the negative emotions – fear and hate – labeling them "the ways of the dark side."

The sci-fi/action film trilogy *The Matrix*, first released in 1999, follows the same lead with the main character Neo (played by actor Keanu Reeves) trying to discover if he is "The One." In a scene where Neo is supposed to leap from one building top to another, the character Morpheus (played by actor Laurence Fishburne) tells the young trainee, "You've got to let it all go, Neo – fear, doubt and disbelief. Free your mind." Science fiction? Yes. But take a closer look.

In 1902, two brothers took on a mission that seemed impossible to the world. What they proposed was straight out of a science fiction movie – to create an object that could shackle the air and fly in the sky like a bird.

The two brothers of course were Wilbur and Orville Wright. The doubters were plentiful. A flying machine made no sense. It was "foolish" to believe such a feat could be accomplished. At times the aircraft would stay in the air for only 12 seconds before crashing, but that was no deterrent to the Wright brothers. They stayed the course.

They *knew* what they were attempting could somehow be done. Some mechanism in their brains was receiving a transmission that said, "Keep trying, you're almost there." While many would have quit because of what appeared to be failure, those pioneers continued on to accomplish their mission. On Dec. 17, 1903, at Kitty Hawk, NC, those two chosen souls flew in their aircraft.

The Secret To Knowing Is "Trust"

Have you ever been thinking of someone and out of the blue that person called you? You picked up the phone and couldn't believe your ears. In disbelief you said, "You're not going to believe this . . . I was just thinking about you."

Most people laugh it off and don't think much of it. They chalk it up to coincidence and leave it at that. But the more evolved recognize the full meaning of the occurrence. The Bible allegorically refers to that process in Ecclesiastes 10:20: *"For the bird of the air will carry the voice, and that which hath wings will tell the matter."*

Thought is a very powerful source of energy, and it travels. The concentrated energy that emanates from one person's thoughts sends an electrical impulse that is picked up by your mental receiver. Since we weren't taught how that part of our brain functions, it is difficult for most to *trust* what we experience.

Even though a person may experience that phenomenon many times, he still can't quite believe it. Each time it happens, he chalks it up to coincidence. The moment he stops discounting the experience and starts trusting his faculties, he will experience an element of *knowing*.

Most people balk at things they consider "supernatural." They place those things in the sci-fi classification and don't put much trust in them. Upon closer observation of the words "supernatural," you will discover how closely they describe who we are.

Let's replace the words "super" with big and "natural" with nature. In other words, you and I are big in nature. We are supernatural beings. Everything about being body and spirit, at the same time, is supernatural.

From this moment on, open your mind to the total picture of who you are. Do not minimize your earthly experience by viewing yourself exclusively through finite terms. Think outside the box, and call upon every power available to you. If you are to be a master on this planet, you must be prepared to "boldly go where no man/woman has gone before."

The Hidden 90%

It's been said we use only 10% of our brains. We've heard it so much, many of us have grown immune to what that really means. If you use only 10% of your brain (at most) and you have 100% at your disposal, the obvious question should be, "How do I access the other 90%?"

Albert Einstein said, "Imagination is your world, it's a preview of things to come." Einstein understood one of the great mysteries of the human equation. He understood the greater part of who you are resides in the imagination realm.

This physical world vibrates at a much slower rate than the imagination realm. In this world, things are solid and concentrated. To make use of objects on the physical level, energy must connect in a way that allows us to touch it.

Those things that exist in the imagination realm are just as real as the things we touch in the physical realm – they just exist in another medium. Since none of us took an "Imagination Development" class in school, it is difficult to understand how to take advantage of our imagination power.

Every creation in life happened twice – once in the imagination realm and secondly on the physical canvas. The greats understood how that dynamic worked and generously tapped into the secret forces.

You, too, have the capacity to draw from the greatest source known to man and bring forth results that are miraculous. All you have to do is listen differently. Life constantly is talking to you.

You probably can recall times when you imagined living a greater life than you currently enjoy. You could see all aspects of your new life in detail. The thought seemed so real you wanted to pursue it but instead talked yourself out of it. A moment later you were thrust back into reality and chalked it up to your imagination.

Those pictures you discard are real. They merely exist in another realm. As you begin to trust yourself and operate in a state of knowing, you will call upon that information and use it to create at an optimum level.

The other 90% of your brain you've been looking for resides in your imagination, the virtual "untapped" zone of the infinite. That's where you will find the secrets of the universe and the blueprint to your destiny.

That may sound like "hocus pocus" to you, but take a look for yourself. What movies have captured the greatest audiences? What books stand as classics? What pieces of art captivate the mind and senses? What songs touch the spirit and move the soul?

You will discover the answers to those questions are those that seem to come from the universe itself. When a great singer sings a song, it's as if she goes into a trance and allows the song to flow through her. It seems as if she closes her eyes and draws from a greater source. A painter was known to say, "I let the paintbrush go and let the universe fill the canvas."

For some, that information will be too "way-out" and thus won't reach their subconscious mind where action takes place. For others, that information will set them on a course of discovery. Both will end up where they were intended to be.

Overcoming Obstacles

Mastering the art of knowing will allow you to move into a state of consciousness that commands results. No longer will you have to see results first before you act. You will know the thing you are looking for already exists, and armed with that knowledge, you merely move toward it.

Operating in a state of knowing allows you to understand time frames. You understand the natural process of *thought and creation.* You understand the illusion of your dream never coming true is just that – an "illusion."

It's like the previous example in which you pictured yourself traveling to a distant city. Even though you don't see it in your current reality, your destination is moving toward you as fast as you are moving toward it.

Here's an easy way to predict your future. Ask yourself, "What did I do today to make my dream of tomorrow come true" The answer will allow you to see your tomorrow. In other words, your future is being shaped by what you do each moment.

Use the illustration of the distant city to understand the *creation* process. When you set out to travel from one city to another, you automatically allot a certain amount of time to reach your destination. You then get into your vehicle, point yourself in the right direction and begin the journey. You *know* it will be only a matter of time before you reach your destination.

Because you understand the way that process works as it relates to traveling, you do not get frustrated by how much time it takes to travel from one city to the next. Manifesting your dream follows the same formula. You first set your course to your objective. You then prepare a route to your dream, checking to make sure you're on course. And last, you allow time for your dream to come into view.

Taking the Guesswork Out of Success

The noted German sociologist Georg Simmel made the following statement, "If one asserts that one 'can' do something, then this means not only the mental anticipation of future events, but an already existing state of energy, physical and psychic coordination's."

That's a very profound statement – one that also describes the essence of "knowing." In other words, if you say you know something, you must be able to go touch it right now or know where it is and how to get to it and be able to replicate that action at will. For instance, if you own a car, you can say, "I know I can go open the door to my car." That occurrence is not the mere anticipation of a future event; it is the already existing energies, physical and psychic coordination's.

Reaching your dreams requires that amount of knowing, which allows you to call upon the necessary energies to turn your dreams into reality. When you can say, "I know where my dream is and how I am going to get to it," you will be closer to realizing that goal.

To put it in simple terms, knowing is like a business plan. The reason a bank asks an aspiring entrepreneur to draft a plan is to make sure he knows all the ends and outs about his business. It also allows the potential investor to troubleshoot any business problems or weaknesses.

The bank does not want to take a risk on merely a good idea – it wants to "know" there is a high probability of recouping its investment.

When you take the time to do the work and invest the time to gain self-mastery, you will "know" beyond a shadow of doubt what you are capable of producing. Obtaining your dream will be secondary to your exhaustive preparation.

Know Your Way to Success

To attain and maintain a knowing consciousness requires practice. Taking some time each day to feel and experience your *knowing* will create the habit of operating in a *state of knowing*. That is not an accidental or coincidental conscious level.

Any discipline that allows you to exert an element of control over yourself or your world requires a concentrated daily, hourly, moment-by-moment awareness action. You must be mindful of the seeds of doubt that penetrate and permeate your consciousness with every thought you shape. The doubt process is to your *knowing* as weeds are to a farmer's garden.

Knowing creates urgency. Imagine winning the lottery. You just left the lottery office, and it's confirmed you won $10 million. Your check will be ready in two days. Now picture your preparation. Picture the feeling in your heart. How long would it take you to buy that car or truck you've only dreamed about up to that point? Can you feel your initial sense of urgency – the excitement that comes with knowing all your dreams have come true?

Knowing leads to action. Picture waking up on day two after winning the lottery (if you could have slept at all) – this is the day $10 million is waiting for you. Can you see yourself preparing to pick up the check? What if the car wouldn't start? Would that prevent you from getting to the lottery office to claim your check? What if no one you called would give you a ride? What would you do? I think you get the point. Even if you had to walk to the lottery office, you would take the necessary action to get there. As a matter of fact, you would head to the office skipping and singing. Knowing leads to action – even in the face of adversity.

UNBELIEVABLE! That's what your future looks like when you operate in a state of knowing.

*"To find a career to which you are
adapted by nature and then to work hard at it,
is about as near a formula for success
and happiness as the world provides."*

Mark Sullivan

– STAGE THREE –
WORTH REMEMBERING

- Turning your personal value into its monetary equivalent will require a greater-than-ordinary effort.

- You must be able to generate the necessary amount of energy that allows others to see you as a marketable product.

- When you operate in a state of knowing, you see through obstacles. You become one with your mission, and even the most trying circumstances are no match for your inner-resolve.

- The conscious level of knowing is the final frontier for any power broker determined to reach new heights and snatch victory from the hands of defeat.

- Only three of the 100 said, "I will." Those three had the mindset that produces victory. I call it the "knowing mindset."

- Knowing leaves no room for anything except action.

- Knowing is a deep internal belief that comes from experiencing something in a tangible manner. It is the feeling you get when you put in the work and have total belief in the outcome.

- Any discipline that allows you to exert an element of control over you or your world requires a concentrated daily, hourly, moment-by-moment awareness action.

- Here's an easy way to predict your future. Ask yourself, "What did I do today to make my dream of tomorrow come true?" The answer will allow you to see your tomorrow.

STAGE 4
DEVELOPING RELATIONSHIPS

Connect The Dots to Your Success

– STAGE FOUR –

*Who you know may get you in the door,
but it's what you know that keeps you there.*

We Shall 217

THE POWER
OF NETWORKING

Increasing Your Scope of Influence

One of my favorite movie lines was uttered by a character in the 1990 film *The Godfather III*: "The richest among you is he with the most powerful friends." That line carries a great truth – one every power player must learn and master.

Your ability to garner the wealth you desire is in part derived from the contacts you amass. The quality of those contacts dictates your influence. The amount of influence you wield increases your personal value. And your personal value directly influences your status in life.

The No. 1 rule to power networking is, "Bring something to the table." Your ability to effectively network with individuals who can assist you in reaching your desired level of success is based on what you personally have to offer.

Every power broker paid his dues to get to where he is. His close associates also have paid their dues to attain their status. The question is, "What noteworthy accomplishments do you bring to the table that will gain you admittance to the group?" You must be able to answer that question with a positive response.

Networking follows a basic rule, "Get in where you fit in." The worst thing you can do in the scope of networking is to try to be where you're not ready to be. Never try to force your way into a situation just because you desire to be there. The result can be devastating.

Allow your growth to be natural. Each new hurdle you overcome will grant you the name power required to bring you before powerful people. As you continue to grow, your fame will increase and the recognition of your power will cause doors to automatically open.

Developing Your Support System

Your networking strategy should encompass a foundation of local support first. Who are the power players in your immediate environment? Do you have access to them? What do they know about you and your talents?

An effective route to meeting and connecting with individuals of influence is increasing the languages you speak. By languages I mean activities. How's your golf game? Golf is a language. If you don't believe me, ask a golfer about his handicap or his last round. The more activities or disciplines you master, the easier your ability to interact with those you wish to befriend.

Join local and national organizations. People do business with people they know and like. When you join an organization, you gain access to an entire group of people and processes. By being a member, you gain common ground with others who can be of benefit to you and your end objective.

Getting Your Foot In The Door

The person you dream of networking and doing business with has an executive assistant. Do you know her name? Do you know any other information about her such as job responsibilities, hobbies or family background? Keep in mind, the person who answers the office telephone is as important to you as the business leader you wish to impact.

The mistake many people make, as it relates to networking, is overlooking key people who are crucial to their success. Most individuals get so fixated on getting to "The Big Man" they bypass steps that could make their journey easier.

It would be wise to remember the executive assistant who answers the phone for "The Big Man" probably has his ear more than anyone else in his immediate world. She knows how he feels when he enters the office and can tell you the best way to approach him about a particular subject – if she likes you.

The art of taking a moment and connecting with the assistant is more valuable than you know. Most calls she takes on a daily basis are from people who treat her as an answering machine. She answers the phone, receives the information, takes a message and ends the call.

Think of how refreshing it would be if someone actually greeted her with, "Hello, how is your day going?" She probably would think it was a "personal" call. Someone actually wants to know how she's doing?

If she is worth her salt (which she probably is – that's how she got to be "The Big Man's" right hand), her allegiance will be to her boss first, but since you took time to acknowledge her, she may give you a tidbit of inside info.

Never let your networking include only "prominent people." If you do, you will miss the mark. Recognize and respect the process that leads to those prominent doors. Remember there are six degrees of separation that connect you to anybody on the planet. Be wise and learn how to connect the dots.

The Higher You Climb

Allow me to extend an ounce of caution. You can take this with a grain of salt, but believe me, it has merit – people are better equipped to take advantage of you the higher you climb in life.

People who make it to the top easily recognize a "newbie" who desperately wants to get into the inner circle. The newbie's eagerness is written across his forehead, and it generally reads, "I'll do anything – just let me in!"

They'll let you in all right – rather they'll let "your money" in. Before long, they will invite you to participate in network marketing schemes where you have to recruit a zillion people to make some money.

You can't get in for free either; they want your cash upfront. You figure it's a small price to pay for admission. That couldn't be further from the truth. If you get entangled in one of those networking relationships, you will discover when your money runs out, so does the networking.

With that in mind, allow your networking to evolve naturally. Networking relationships are like friendships – they should be chosen carefully. It is far easier to get into a destructive business relationship than to get out of one. By all means, be careful.

Networking – Not "Favor Asking"

A great inhibitor to networking is asking for favors. People do favors for people they do business with, but that should not be the only reason you communicate with someone. If your scope of networking is calling on someone when you need something, you will miss the mark.

True networking occurs when both parties benefit from one another. If you have power in your local market and have access to businesses and opportunities, you are of value to someone in another market.

The art of networking comes from your ability to open your market to the other person and vice versa. Through effective networking, you can increase your influence and attract an ally at the same time.

Another critical aspect of networking is follow-up. Take time to communicate "informally" with the person with whom you want to network. You can do that through e-mails, phone calls or sending newspaper clippings of interest.

The art of the deal is to develop a relationship. Take time and discover the likes and dislikes of the person you're networking with. Talk to him about his hobbies, career and future goals. Identify ways to get together for business or social events. Keep in mind, the greater the familiarity, the greater the bond, and the greater the bond, the more natural it will be to do business.

K.I.S.S – Keep It Simple, Stupid! Most people associate with other people for two reasons – what they can get and how much more they can get. If you can provide one of those things, they gladly will hang out with you.

If you don't believe that assertion, think about why you hang out with people. Whether it's a lady friend, guy friend, co-worker or higher-up, you want something out of the time you spend together. Even if it's pleasant conversation you seek, you want something. Keep that in mind when you identify someone you want to network with.

Landing the Big Fish – Power Borrowing

As you climb the ladder of success, it is important you gain access to power. Since you are new to the game, you don't possess the "name power" needed to garner national attention. You must learn the art of "power borrowing." To add power to your name, you must know how to land "the big fish."

Every field of business has top individuals who represent the pinnacle of success. Those people have name recognition and are hailed as stars of their industry. In music, for example, Jay-Z represents hip-hop. When it comes to computers, you generally think Microsoft and Bill Gates. And in the field of investing and money, Warren Buffet's name comes to mind.

As an up-and-coming power broker, you can increase your power and gain access to closed doors by partnering with a well-known name. Most people don't think it's possible to get a celebrity to help them with their careers, so they never even try to approach someone famous.

One thing that helped me climb to the top of my career was gaining assistance from Les Brown, world-renowned speaker and best-selling author. After listening to his motivational tapes, I decided to write him a letter in 1995.

One day thereafter, while sitting at the house, I received a phone call from Les. I was amazed he called me. It was quite unbelievable, and he could tell from my reaction I was blown away.

Les and I have so much in common, it's uncanny. Our birthdays are on the same day, and Les has a twin brother named Wesley. I told him, "You've been calling my name all your life. We were meant to find each other."

The fact that I took time to write Les and acknowledge the impact he had on my life prompted him to follow up with me. Since then, we have worked together and shared meals, and he wrote a powerful testimonial on the back cover of this book.

My personal relationship with a multimillion-dollar power broker has opened many doors for me. I gain immediate recognition just by placing his name next to mine. When I tell people I received my professional speaker's training from Les Brown, those who know his credentials listen to me with an attentive ear.

The basic rule to landing a big fish is make sure you have a solid foundation before you contact the mentor. That means you have to possess a degree of accomplishment if a power broker is to take you seriously.

The reason is a power broker often is approached by people who want him/her to do all the work and make them rich. People of power don't have time for that. However, a power broker may be willing to advise a business person ready for success and only needs a door opened to be victorious.

A power broker who remembers the time someone opened the door for him/her may be eager to assist you. When your preparation reaches the point where it is purpose-driven, start looking for the power broker who can open that door you cannot open yourself. Power recognizes power, and your tenacious work on your career will create recognizable power.

Make Your Interest
Other People's Interest

One of the greatest mistakes entrepreneurs make early on in their careers is putting their interest before the interest of others. What I mean by that is they get infected with "I-itis."

The "I-itis" disease affects their vision and only allows them to see their own needs. You can recognize the symptoms of the disease by listening to their sales pitch. It generally goes something like this, "I want you to help me with my project. I think what I created is really great, and I can see myself going national with this product. This is a great way for you to give back for all life has done for you by helping me . . . "

People in positions of power hear pitches like that every day. They listen and yawn, check their watches and wait for their assistant to tell them it's time for the next meeting (as the assistant were instructed to do before you arrived).

The art of the deal is to make your interest other people's interest. You can do that by identifying who would most benefit from your service or product. For example, a friend of mine created a music program. He found out a local nonprofit organization needed to increase its arts programs. He approached the organization's leaders and told them he could help them meet "their" objective. They embraced him with open arms. Both parties walked away happy because "both" got what they *needed*.

*"It takes TEAMWORK to make
the DREAM WORK."*

George Fraser

– STAGE FOUR –
WORTH REMEMBERING

- "The richest among you is he with the most powerful friends."

- Your ability to garner the wealth you desire is in part derived from the contacts you amass.

- The No. 1 rule to power networking is, "Bring something to the table."

- Never try to force your way into a situation just because you desire to be there.

- Who are the power players in your immediate environment? Do you have access to them? What do they know about you and your talents?

- The more activities or disciplines you master, the easier your ability to interact with those you wish to befriend.

- Each person you come in contact with is a doorway to a vast world of opportunities.

- The mistake many people make, as it relates to networking, is overlooking key people who are crucial to their success.

- People are more equipped to take advantage of you the higher you climb in life.

- Networking relationships are like friendships – they should be chosen carefully.

STAGE 5
BUILDING CAPACITY

Developing Character

– STAGE FIVE –

"People only see what they are prepared to see."
Ralph Waldo Emerson

PREPAREDNESS

To "Know" Is To Prepare

A new and exciting world is opening for you. The possibilities are endless. New people, new energies and new opportunities are beginning to avail themselves to you. As you begin to operate in a state of knowing, you start to consciously accept the new world you are creating. In so doing, you realize the new life you are seeking is moving toward you right now. Faced with that knowledge, you *prepare*.

Mental Fortitude

The physical act of winning is secondary to the mental preparation. To succeed at any level, an exhaustive mental conditioning must come first. The monetary reward you obtain will reflect the mental picture in your "third-eye view."

Your "third-eye view" is better known as your subconscious mind, and that is where your "real" desires exist. Regardless of the hype you put into the creation of wealth, the final outcome will in part be dictated by what you expect to receive. Your daily life actions result from information retained in your "third-eye view" – where the "real you" resides. Whatever reaches that mental compartment becomes reality, even if it doesn't make sense to anyone else on the planet.

Noah and the Ark

Remember the Biblical story *Noah and the Ark* in which Noah was warned of the great flood of 40 days and 40 nights before it happened? Picture how foolish Noah must have appeared to his neighbors while building the ark.

Nothing in the weather conditions foretold the need to prepare to the extent Noah was. I imagine he was the laughing stock of the community. He was forewarned of the great flood and began to prepare accordingly. When the rain did come, Noah was prepared.

Noted author Earl Nightingale writes about a time when he was a disc jockey at a small radio station. Each time he created a commercial at the small station, he made it sound like a major market production. "The other disc jockeys laughed and made fun of me," he recalled. They thought he was full of himself and putting too much work into those small commercials.

Soon he left that small station and landed a job at one of the largest stations in the country. He was preparing all along for the success he knew would be his one day. Even though his early preparation looked foolish to his peers, he stayed true to his inner vision. His preparation paid off, and he enjoyed the last laugh.

Your ability to see your future will affect your ability to properly prepare for it. Whereas before you felt you had what it took to make your dreams come true, you now will know you have what it takes. Operating with a newfound sense of certainty, you will begin to "actively" prepare.

Actively Prepare

You can look to all areas of your life and discover the extent of your knowing simply by identifying what you are *actively* preparing for. To actively prepare means you are taking the required steps, at the required time, to meet an established deadline.

What are you actively preparing for? The answer will be very revealing – it may be "to launch my new business" or "to position myself for a higher position in the company." If it is difficult to answer that question, you may lack the knowing necessary to move to a state of preparation.

If you do not have a plan for your life, you will not generate the energy and focus that will enable you to prepare accordingly. Preparation, therefore, comes as a result of knowing.

The lack of knowing is one of the central elements that leads to procrastination. The inability to see with clarity the end result of your efforts stops you from mounting a sustained concentrated initiative required to bring it to fruition.

Even though you start a project all fired up and ready to conquer the world, your energies may wane when unforeseen obstacles and challenges occur. Something as trivial as another person's doubt can halt the most attainable dream.

The Antidote to Fear

The fear component in the central nervous system is triggered when you face a situation you assume you cannot control. Some situations are real, however, others are figments of your imagination.

If you use your imagination to view the outcome of a future situation, you may encounter fear. Your mind can conjure up multiple reasons why you probably will have a negative encounter. It is amazing how the mind can create countless scenarios that all end with you failing.

Absent of the proper preparation, your imagination can become a fierce adversary. Instead of being your internal partner, it acts against you and paralyzes your efforts. When you prepare to the degree required to withstand your challenges, your imagination becomes your ally.

As your ally, your imagination conjures up pictures of you succeeding. You find yourself ready to meet challenges head-on with confidence and positive expectations. Therefore, the antidote to fear is preparation.

With proper preparation, you will build a defense against things that threaten you. You must learn to picture future events and circumstances and prepare accordingly. For instance, you may be asked to speak before a group. By knowing the date of the event and the subject matter, you can begin to prepare. The framework of your preparation will consist of researching your topic, crafting your message and practicing your speech.

The art you must master is seeing the future, experiencing the fear and systematically preparing against that fear. If you know you have a problem getting started with your presentation, the best course of action is to prepare a strong beginning. If you have a problem at the end of your presentation, work on a strong close. Experiencing the fear before it occurs allows you to mount a proactive approach that guards against it.

NASA astronauts are the best at putting that practice to use. For months they perform simulated tests in a controlled environment. They experience the feeling of weightlessness and every other nuance associated with space travel. As a matter of fact, when one of the astronauts finally walked on the moon, he said it felt like he thought it would – just like the simulator.

Prepare - Prepare - PREPARE!

Whitney M. Young Jr. was right when he said, *"It is better to be prepared for an opportunity and not have one, than to have an opportunity, and not be prepared." What is your greatest dream for your life? What hidden desire do you want to become reality? Whatever it is, you can be sure the opportunity will arise for it to occur. The question is "Will you be prepared?"*

The act of visualization, when properly applied, can bring to the surface the exact emotions experienced in real life. Your ability to live those feelings before they occur will strengthen your resolve and prepare you for greater success.

Whatever you want to do in life requires preparation. You must prepare yourself for the greatness you one will day realize. The bigger the feat, the greater the desire and the *greater the preparation.*

"To follow, without halt, one aim:
There's the key to success."

Anna Pavlova

– STAGE FIVE –
WORTH REMEMBERING

- The physical act of winning is secondary to the mental preparation.

- The monetary reward you obtain will reflect the mental picture in your "third-eye view."

- Regardless of the hype you put into the creation of wealth, the final outcome will in part be dictated by what you expect to receive.

- You can look to all areas of your life and discover the extent of your *knowing* simply by identifying what you are *actively* preparing for.

- To actively prepare means you are taking the required steps, at the required time, to meet an established deadline.

- If you do not have a plan for your life, you will not generate the energy and focus that will enable you to prepare accordingly. Preparation, therefore, comes as a result of knowing.

- The art you must master is seeing the future, experiencing the fear and systematically preparing against that fear.

- The act of visualization, when properly applied, can bring to the surface the exact emotions experienced in real life.

- Your ability to live those feelings before they occur will strengthen your resolve and prepare you for greater success.

STAGE 6
PROPER REPETITION

Developing Winning Habits

– STAGE SIX –

*A constant dripping of water
wears through the greatest boulder –
no obstacle can withstand consistency.*

We Shall 217

THE POWER
OF CONSISTENCY

Never Give Up!

It is no coincidence the same companies topped the Fortune 500 list the past five years. They remain at the top through continued innovation and a solid understanding of the power of consistency. Major conglomerates understand the destruction that follows complacency. They realize they will fail if they rest on their laurels and count on past successes and market positions.

For that reason, every major corporation has a research and development department. Through the department's initiatives, large companies stay alert to new trends or increase their market share with the expansion of current products and services.

Companies determined to stay at the top understand "the dinosaur analogy." They recognize the largest animal on Earth one day can be non-existent the next.

Guaranteed Results

When you master consistency, you guarantee results. Just as a continual dripping of water wears through the greatest boulder, your consistent actions also will wear through any and all obstacles.

The key is consistency. You cannot be effective with a hit-and-miss approach. You must train yourself to focus and remain consistent. Your actions must evolve into habits, and your consistent habits will lead you to your appointed destiny.

No longer will you worry about losing weight or saving money. You merely will set your course and place your "mental dial" on *consistent*. Once your dial is set, you don't have to look in the mirror or watch your account for growth. Just continue doing the action. And when you finally look up, you will have arrived at your destination.

When you observe those who have amassed billions of dollars, you recognize they understand and incorporate consistency into their game plan. Billionaire Warren Buffet is known for consistently picking winning stocks. Billionaire Bill Gates consistently produces cutting-edge technology or hires individuals who assist him to do so. Media icon Oprah Winfrey consistently is growing her empire by producing television and movie projects, publishing a magazine and creating a radio program.

It is easy to attain a certain status, but the difficultly lies in maintaining it. The secret to sustained performance is "where you set your sights." The person who sets his sights on just "getting there" may reach his objective but won't have a plan beyond that point. On the other hand, the individual who sees beyond the point of victory, and plans accordingly, increases his chances of sustained progress.

Greatness

"He's done it again! Can you believe it?!
That's what makes him great!"

We've heard it over and over again. We've come to expect it – adulation, endless superlatives, shouts and screams when the great ones do the unbelievable again!

"Three, two, one – Michael scores!"
"It's on the way, yes! Another championship for Tiger."
"He's down! Foreman is down! Unbelievable!
Ali just knocked out invincible George Foreman!"

Many are called, but few enter the ranks of the great. History has opened and closed the door on those who had what it took to attain success but not what it took to sustain it. Remember Vanilla Ice or Hammer? Maybe Buster Douglas? Each shined brightly for the moment, only to flicker and fade after their brilliant encounter with fame.

Doing the Seemingly Impossible – Again and Again

What will make you shine your brightest? It's the very thing that makes the great ones great. Consistency! If Michael Jordan made every basket during the game but consistently missed the game-winning shot, he would be remembered as good but not great. If Tiger Woods won the Masters by a whopping 12 strokes and only won sparingly after that, he would be known as *good* but not *great*. The ability to do the seemingly impossible, time and time again, is what separates the *good* from the *great*.

Vince Lombardi said, "For winners, winning is not an event – it's a habit." Winners are used to winning. They are highly competitive on and off the playing field. They understand there are no shortcuts to victory; the only way to out-distance your opponent is to consistently work harder than he does.

Winners bask in the excitement and praise they receive from their worthy accomplishment and look forward to experiencing that feeling again.

The Byproduct of a Made-Up Mind

The dynamic energies contained in consistency are the byproducts of a made-up mind. Can you recall a time when you were committed to making a change in your life? There probably were two prevalent factors: 1) You were plain fed-up with who you were 2) You were determined to have something better and would not be denied.

Maybe it was something as simple as losing weight (which isn't really simple at all) or getting your body in shape for summer. Take a moment and perform the following exercise. At its completion, you will discover you have been given one of the most powerful tools imaginable in relationship to achieving success. You will have to put the book down for a moment to complete this exercise.

Dream-Making Energy

Write down an experience when you were determined to do something and would not be denied. First picture the event in your mind. Concentrate on how you felt once you decided you were not going to take no for an answer. For this exercise, the experience can be negative or positive. Remembering the occurrence in detail will allow you to discover the workings of what I call "Dream-Making Energy (DME)." Are you ready? Do the exercise now.

I hope you didn't just skip the exercise. If you did, that's fine. Maybe you will come back to it later. If you participated, I've got great news for you! In the information you just wrote down is the secret that will add yet another piece to the puzzle to bring you the success you seek. Take a look again at what you wrote. You'll notice an interesting occurrence.

Immediately after you identified what you wanted to do, energy was created. Stop! Make your mind only focus on that energy. Can you remember it? Take your time and really go over the experience in detail.

You will recall you first identified the object or occurrence you wanted. You then placed your mind (your total mind) on it. You may remember you thought about what could stop you from getting what you wanted. If you did think about it, you instantly decided, "So what!" You knew you would not be denied! The moment you said, "So what!," an even greater energy emerged.

That energy is the raw universal material that makes dreams reality. It is equivalent to the electricity that runs your lights or appliances. That pure electrical energy is what turns a loser into a winner and a winner into a giant!

Winners continue to win and are able to bounce back when they fall because they understand how to shackle DME. When winners are up, they use DME to sustain their flight. When winners are down, they use DME to carry them back to where they were before the fall. You see the reality of that principle in successful people who have made millions, went broke and made millions again.

The ability to harness DME will bring you everything you seek and desire. If you are to achieve the success you seek, you must develop an understanding of that force and how it operates. Think about the electricity in your home. The smaller appliances require smaller amounts of electricity to operate. Now consider the wattage necessary to run a major rock 'n' roll concert.

Achievement of your dreams follows the same principle. Smaller accomplishments may require the shackling of a smaller amount of DME. The larger the project, dream or aspiration, the larger and more concentrated the DME required to make it a reality.

Do not discount the importance of this exercise. Use the example you wrote as an instrument to teach yourself how to come into contact with that creative energy. Feel free to upgrade your experience. If you think of an experience where you went to a great length to obtain a prize and would not be denied, use that one. Make sure the example you use is one where you actually obtained the prize you sought.

You will discover the greater the odds against getting something you would not be denied, the greater the production of DME. Dream-Making Energy is the fuel that exists between the thought and the achievement. Understanding how to use that universal energy will allow you to reach your goals at the maximum rate of speed – Godspeed.

Consistency Breeds Trust

Who are the people who earn our greatest trust? They are the individuals who consistently keep their word to us. They are the individuals we know we can count on in crunch time. Our trust is gained by things, situations or people who produce the same results over the course of time. We call that consistency.

When you check the record books, you will find those who attained success in any discipline had certain words that characterized them. Words like tenacious, hard-working, courageous, determined, go-getter, committed, driven, ambitious and competitive. The word consistent stands above all those superlatives.

If you want to impress your peers, all you have to do is stay true to a course of action when everyone else has given up. Rarely will you meet an individual who stayed committed to his dream long enough for it to materialize.

When you stay committed to your dream, others will begin to trust your belief in it. They will recognize you are in it for the long haul and your dream is not a fleeting fancy. They will understand your committed efforts have allowed you to gain a certain mastery of your craft, and they will begin to call upon your services in that capacity.

A person who is consistent is a rare breed. We live in a "ready-mix, get-rich-quick" world where instant gratification is the rule of the day. When you decide to take on the ways of consistency, you prepare yourself to meet with greatness.

"Look at a stone cutter cutting away at his rock, perhaps a hundred times without as much as a crack showing in it. Yet at the hundred-and-first blow it will split in two. I know it was not the last blow that did it, but all that had gone before."

Jacob Riis

– STAGE SIX –
WORTH REMEMBERING

- It is no coincidence the same companies topped the Fortune 500 list the past five years.

- Major conglomerates understand the destruction that follows complacency. They realize they will fail if they rest on their laurels and count on past successes and market positions.

- They recognize "the dinosaur analogy" – the largest animal on Earth one day can be non-existent the next.

- The ability to do the seemingly impossible, time and time again, is what separates the *good* from the *great.*

- The initial feeling of exhilaration that comes from the first win paves the way for future victories.

- Consistency takes knowing to an entirely different level.

- Consistency + *knowing* = **results!**

- The dynamic energies contained in consistency are the byproducts of a made-up mind.

- Dream-Making Energy (DME) is the fuel that exists between the thought and the achievement.

- Understanding how to use that universal energy will allow you to reach your goals at the maximum rate of speed – Godspeed.

STAGE 7
DISCOVER
YOUR CALLING

Walking The Talk

– STAGE SEVEN –

*"There are two great days in a person's life –
the day we are born
and the day we discover why."*
William Barclay

THE MOTIVATING
POWER OF PURPOSE

Live Life with Passion

Purpose is the one thing in life that makes you go the extra mile when you are dead tired, helps you get back up when you fall in front of people and keeps you moving forward when others don't believe in you anymore.

Much has been written about the power of purpose, but most people are no closer to finding theirs than they are to winning the lottery. It's one of those subjects that sounds good but always seems to relate to someone else.

Well, I've got news for you. If you plan to live a life of excitement, passion and adventure, you would be wise to find a purpose to fulfill. It is purpose that excites, ignites, drives, empowers and pulls you to heights you only have imagined.

Having a purpose to draw upon makes you "superhuman." How else do you think anti-apartheid leader Nelson Mandela of South Africa turned down freedom after serving 25 of his eventual 27 years in prison?   He told his capturers if freedom was a question of compromising his purpose, "Thanks, but no thanks."

How else do you think the Rev. Martin Luther King Jr. allowed himself to be jailed and stoned and never turned to violence? It would have been easy for him to grow bitter after witnessing the evil and vile side of humanity. His purpose gave him focus and pulled him forward to victory.

You may say that kind of purpose is not for you. And you probably are right. Not everyone is on Earth to perform those extraordinary tasks, however, the purpose you choose will allow you to draw upon that kind of power.

Finding Your Purpose

The obvious question is, "How do I find my purpose?" One way is to recognize the possibility there is a reason for your existence. By recognizing that possibility, you start seeing yourself differently. You stop being a walking accident and become a factual occurrence.

Next, start thinking of causes that spark your interest. Are there any activities in your city, state or nation that appeal to you? Something that continues to capture your attention may be a sign you need to give it more attention.

Consider this: There are no coincidences in an ordered universe. What I mean by that is everything happens for a reason. Everything you are doing now is leading you to where you are supposed to be. Your task is to learn the secrets buried in your current learning experience. When you complete that task, you will graduate to the next level of your development.

Understand this: You must learn all you are to learn in your current capacity before graduating to the next level. You can compare this process to school. You can't advance to the second grade until you pass first.

In order to help others, you must first master yourself. You must rid yourself of any fear that can inhibit your growth. You must become more than selfish wanting. You must become a grand idea. Only then can you reach your maximum potential and edify others.

Picture yourself being led by life to a magical place. Since you don't know where life is leading you, all you can do is follow. As an efficient follower, you have to be where life places you – with exactness. You must be present in the moment – at all times. Only then can you fully understand what life is showing you.

Soon a pattern will emerge, and you will begin to openly recognize your talents and gifts. Because you adhered to life's instructions and understood the significance of each task, you unlike most will find your way to your purpose.

Your purpose is birthed out of each and every life lesson you *fully* engage in. The reoccurrence of victories associated with your skills will spell out the direction you are to go. Having fully developed your talents and gifts, you will be ready to bring to the world the power of your purpose.

Purpose Makes Obstacles Insignificant

In your pursuit to build an empire, you will encounter failure after failure. Failure is as synonymous with winning as dieting is to losing weight. You simply cannot achieve greatness without going through the fiery test of life.

In 1974 near the end of his career, Muhammad Ali – the greatest athlete of all time – faced his greatest challenge. He was pitted against George Foreman – the strongest, meanest and most feared heavyweight in the division.

Foreman had just demolished Smokin' Joe Frazier in a recent bout, making Frazier look like a featherweight. Since Foreman beat Frazier so handily and Frazier just beat Ali, boxing analysts and fans doubted that Ali had a chance against "Invincible George."

The fight took place in Zaire, Africa, a place Ali considered home for all black people. Upon arriving in Africa, Ali received a champion's greeting. Thousands of Africans showed up at the airport and began shouting, "Ali, bumaye" (meaning "Ali, kill him").

Seeing those Africans show up and revere him in such a way added to Ali's feeling of purpose. He would deem that fight, "The greatest fight of my life." The fact that he was considered an underdog – for one of the few times in his career – added to his need to show the world his greatness.

Ali said: *"I'm not fighting for prestige, I'm fighting to lift my people who are sleeping on concrete floors in America, black people who can't eat, black people on welfare, black people who don't have no knowledge of themselves, and black people who don't have no future. When I go into the ring – you see the mind I got now – I got a power now. I got a power I'm not even gonna realize, a power I don't even know. I might look at myself and say, 'How did I do that?' – Allah, God – I'm his tool – God got into me – my purpose is for my people – this man looks small now."*

Those around him were less than convinced. They were aware of Foreman's power, and coupled with Ali's pride, they were sure Ali would endure a tremendous beating at the hands of Foreman. But Ali continued to predict his victory.

The rest, of course, is history. Ali knocked out "Invincible George" in the eighth round of the fight. No one could believe it – except Ali, of course. Journalists looked on in amazement, and even Ali's camp was outdone by what he accomplished.

Immediately after Ali's tremendous "purpose-driven" victory, the rains came crashing down. People danced in the streets. Their champion defeated the tyrant, and "symbolically" good triumphed over evil.

The Hidden Lessons of Life

The path to your purpose is through every task you perform. Darwin, through his theory of evolution, stumbled upon a proven fact. Everything evolves into the thing it was intended to be. In other words, the tree – with all its branches and leaves – is in the seed.

We are finite beings. We cannot see beyond the minute in which we live. We can plan for tomorrow, but it is not up to us if tomorrow arrives. Therefore, we can't possibly know how things we experience today factor into the "final" person we are to become.

If you ever watched the movie *The Karate Kid*, you will understand what I mean. In a scene where young Daniel desires to learn karate, Mr. Miyagi assigns him to wash and wax cars. After washing and waxing the cars, the young man grows impatient and tells the instructor he wants to learn karate – not how to wash cars.

The wise instructor tells the young man to acquire a karate stance, and then yells out, "Wax on! Wax off!" To Daniel's surprise, washing and waxing the cars were in fact karate moves. What he thought was trying and boring actually was a lesson in disguise.

You must learn how to watch the things you do in everyday life and attempt to ascertain what skills you are learning while performing those tasks. More importantly, you must do your current-day work to perfection because you don't know what talents "The Master Teacher" is trying to perfect in you.

By perfecting the things you do now, you can advance to the next level of your evolution. Your continued listening and adherence to timing and change will lead you to advancement. Before long, a new picture will emerge, and you will find yourself creating or performing something greater than when you began.

When you don't view your current job as a learning opportunity, you miss out on possible chances to gain valuable insights and experiences that could benefit you further down the line.

Wealth and Purpose

Building a financial empire takes time. It's not something you do overnight. The bigger the empire, the greater the amount of time it will take to build. Your ability to garner and maintain the energy necessary to realize your dream will come through purpose.

Purpose is synonymous with energy. You go to sleep thinking about it, and it wakes you up in the morning refreshed and ready to go. Whereas a job can be exhausting, trivial and demanding, your purpose fits you, draws the best from you and excites you.

Purpose allows you to see a bigger picture than you would see without it. When you pursue your purpose, you draw from the energy of others who see what you see. Together your energies attract more attention, and soon your passion becomes a movement.

Your purpose guides you to the people and places you need to gain the finances to complete your mission. Ask any pioneer who sought to accomplish something big and didn't have the finances to do so, and he will tell you about an intervention that occurred and enabled him to reach his destination.

Berry Gordy Jr., founder of the legendary Motown Records, had a dream of making it big in the music industry. He worked odd jobs to keep money in his pockets, but his love was writing music. His first song that showed promise was "Reet Petite," performed by Jackie Wilson in 1957.

The Gordy family had a system in which the relatives put money in an account and then sought a project they felt worthy of financing. The family didn't think much of Berry's musical pursuits early on, but his tenacity and commitment convinced his relatives to take a chance on him.

With the family money, Berry started Tamla Records and began his history-making journey to Motown fame. He soon signed other artists, and in 1959 Marv Johnson's "You Got What It Takes" became a Top 10 hit.

Detroit was one of the few top markets that didn't have an urban label to support its local talent. Thus, Berry's new creation of Motown Records shot through the roof. His commitment to purpose caused others to see through his eyes and believe in him and his dream. More importantly, it attracted the initial finances he needed to start building his "Motown Empire."

A person with a purpose is such a rare individual that it's difficult to describe. I can say, however, when you encounter such a person, you immediately will recognize him. His impassioned words, direct approach, perseverance and energy will let you know he won't stop until he completes his mission.

Years may pass, and you may wonder what happened to that committed soul. Then out of the blue, you see him on the national or world stage. His purpose attracted the finances he lacked, taking him beyond all obstacles to achieve his dream. Thus, he stands as a testament to the ever-enduring value of purpose.

"WE SHALL'S" TOP 10
PURPOSE-DRIVEN QUOTES

"Where your talents and the needs of the world cross lies your calling."

Aristotle

"Never forget that the purpose for which a man lives is the improvement of the man himself, so that he may go out of this world having, in his great sphere or his small one, done some little good for his fellow creatures and labored a little to diminish the sin and sorrow that are in the world."

William E. Gladstone

"But there is suffering in life, and there are defeats. No one can avoid them. But it's better to lose some of the battles in the struggles for your dreams than to be defeated without ever knowing what you're fighting for."

Paulo Coelho

"Don't waste life in doubts and fears; spend yourself on the work before you, well assured that the right performance of this hour's duties will be the best preparation for the hours and ages that will follow it."

Ralph Waldo Emerson

"That is happiness; to be dissolved into something completely great."

Willa Cather

"The harder the conflict, the more glorious the triumph. What we obtain too cheap, we esteem too lightly; it is dearness only that gives everything its value. I love the man that can smile in trouble, that can gather strength from distress and grow brave by reflection. 'Tis the business of little minds to shrink; but he whose heart is firm, and whose conscience approves his conduct, will pursue his principles unto death."

Thomas Paine

"The greatest use of life is to spend it for something that outlasts it."

William James

"I am here for a purpose and that purpose is to grow into a mountain, not to shrink to a grain of sand. Henceforth will I apply ALL my efforts to become the highest mountain of all and I will strain my potential until it cries for mercy."

Og Mandino

"Here is a test to find out whether your mission in life is complete. If you're alive, it isn't."

Richard Bach

"My mother said to me, 'If you become a soldier, you'll be a general; if you become a monk, you'll end up as the Pope.' Instead, I became a painter and wound up as Picasso."

Pablo Picasso

"*Thought allied fearlessly to purpose becomes creative force: he who knows this is ready to become something higher and stronger than a mere bundle of wavering thoughts and fluctuating sensations; he who does this has become the conscious and intelligent wielder of his mental powers.*"

James Allen

– STAGE SEVEN –
WORTH REMEMBERING

- Purpose is the one thing in life that makes you go the extra mile when you are dead tired, helps you get up when you fall in front of people and keeps you moving forward when others don't believe in you anymore.

- Purpose excites, ignites, drives, empowers and pulls you to heights you only have imagined.

- Having a purpose to draw upon makes you "superhuman."

- You stop being a walking accident and become a factual occurrence.

- Something that continues to capture your attention may be a sign you need to give it more of your attention.

- Another way to view your purpose is simply to adjust the way you see what you currently are doing. Instead of just working a job, try to see it as your purpose.

- The thing he thought was trying and boring – "Wax on! Wax off!" – was in fact a lesson in disguise.

- You must do your current-day work to perfection because you don't know what talents "The Master Teacher" is trying to perfect in you.

STAGE 8
KEEP YOUR EYE ON THE PRIZE

Eliminate Distractions

– STAGE EIGHT –

*Single-mindedness is the **mental zone** reserved for the person who recognizes there is but one acceptable end – success!*
We Shall 217

SINGLE-MINDEDNESS

The Winner's Zone

Unflinching focus – that's the zone where winners reside. A winner is able to block out any and every thing unassociated with his dream. As you prepare to garner the wealth you desire, you would be wise to learn the ways of single-mindedness.

Single-mindedness is vital to your success because of the life distractions you will encounter along the way. Every major undertaking requires extensive contact with a variety of people. Your ability to effectively navigate those waters will rely on your ability to keep your eyes on the prize.

Single-mindedness makes invisible all things not associated with your goal or destination. You probably can recall a time when you were listening to music while working on a project. Somewhere during the process you ceased to hear the music. You only became aware of the music when you exited the realm of single-mindedness.

Focus – Extreme Intensity

The ability to intensely focus can be likened to the lens of a powerful telescope. The lens focuses the power of the sunray coming through the telescope and increases it a thousand times.

In other words, a person using extreme focus can amplify a simple thought a thousand times. You see the reality of that statement through the efforts of George Washington Carver. He discovered 300 different uses for a mere peanut. Again, a simple thought magnified by a thousand.

Your first single-minded effort may be to find your purpose. You can use that as your beginning point. Start by observing yourself at a deeper level. In your mind, retrace the areas of success you've experienced over the course of your life.

When you identify your purpose, you will be ready to zero in on your focus. You may have heard the phrase "eye of the tiger" – that's the level of intensity you must obtain. To develop the eye of the tiger, you must eat, sleep and breathe your purpose.

There can be no separation between you and your purpose. When you go to sleep, you sleep with it. It must be at your fingertips every waking moment of your day. When you sit in front of it, every fiber of your being must respond to it. When you commit your thoughts to it, every other thought must submit to it.

When you focus at that level, you will meet with success. Even if your initial efforts don't produce immediate success, your intense efforts will attract the people, events and opportunities for future victories.

Total Cooperation

Single-mindedness is attained when there is total cooperation between the heart, mind and body. When those three units operate in unison toward one objective, the result will be success.

Mastering that state of mind requires all three faculties to be firing at the same time toward the same end. The absence of any one of the three will spell failure. Each one of those faculties has its own mode of operation and value system.

The heart continuously embraces *feeling* and all things associated with emotions. The body is consumed with the *appetites* of the world – sexuality, food and all aspects of pleasure. The mind is the *reasoning* mechanism – searching and seeking answers to questions posed by its environment or circumstance.

Most of our lives are spent with those three entities warring with one another. Even when we make up our *minds* to head in a certain direction, one of our faculties always seems to not fully agree with the decision. Therefore, we carry out that decision with only a fragment of our true potential.

The intensity generated from a single-minded act is equivalent to a freight train traveling at top speed. Just like the train, a single-minded thought has one objective – to move forward. Only a force that is equal to or greater than that force stands a chance of surviving such an onslaught. That is the impact of single-mindedness.

Going For It All

Picture a million dollars in cash or any object you desire. Keep in mind the desired object must be something you would give your all for. Now picture your prize high above the ground on a ledge. Imagine yourself climbing a 50-foot ladder. You get to the top of the ladder and realize you can't quite reach the prize. In fact, you realize you must stand at the very top of the ladder to see your prize.

Now you're standing at the top with nothing to hold on to (this test is only between you and your prize). The fear is overwhelming, but you don't give up. You fight your fear. You rise up to grab your prize and then realize you still cannot reach it. By now, the prize is in full view.

There it is, and it's yours for the taking. It occurs to you to reach your prize you have to get on your tiptoes. On top of a 50-foot ladder with no support and a cement floor below – on your tip-toes! (Some people just eliminated themselves from reaching their dream.)

You look inside yourself and recognize how far you've come to get here, how many tears you've cried and how many people said you'd never make it. You recall how often you suffered the humiliation of knowing you can when everyone else thinks you cannot. You rise to your tiptoes, hold your breath and reach for the prize.

But you quickly discover even on your tiptoes you can only touch the ledge that holds your prize. By now, the prize has taken on a new dimension. It's not just a pie-in-the-sky dream anymore. No, no, no! It's yours – it's personal – you can feel the adulation you will receive upon capturing the prize. You can feel the pride that comes from earning the respect of your peers. Your Mom and Dad will say, "That's our son (or daughter)!" They'll be so proud when the neighbors speak highly of them because of you.

All this can be yours! But you discover one small obstacle. To obtain the prize, you have to jump to get it. (Still more individuals, a very large group, just eliminated themselves from obtaining their prize.)

The Mind and Heart of A Winner

Now the mind, heart, body and spirit of a winner truly can be seen. For such a rare human, the prize is not a mere prize at all. The prize, although separate in appearance, really is the winner in another form. You see, you won't risk yourself totally for something you merely want. You will, however, merge with what you are. In the words of Les Brown, best-selling author and speaker, *"You don't get out of life what you want; you get out of life what you are."*

In the winner's mind, there is only one course of action. He or she knows life is meaningless without that prize. So there alone on top of the 50-foot ladder stands the winner. And faced with himself, the part of him that awaited this moment comes forward. He eyes the prize and mentally and physically disengages from his fear. He goes into a state of single-mindedness and with one burst of *knowing*, he jumps to capture his *destiny*.

You may ask, "Did he make it back safely to the ladder? Did he reach the prize? Did he die in the process?" The answer is all the same for it is not the outcome of his fear-defying jump that matters. More important is the fact he jumped – that separates him from his peers and forever makes him "one" among many.

That single-minded act separates winners from the pack. Success is scary because not only must you do all you can to reach the top, but also to make it to the highest level, *you must abandon your fears and jump!*

"Do or do not – there is no try."

**Yoda – character in the
1977 movie *Star Wars***

YOU ARE THE MONEY!

– STAGE EIGHT –
WORTH REMEMBERING

- Single-mindedness is the *mental zone* reserved for the person who recognizes there is only one acceptable end – success!

- A winner is able to block out any and every thing not associated with his dream.

- Single-mindedness is vital to your success because of the life distractions you encounter along the way.

- A person with extreme focus can amplify a simple thought a thousand times.

- George Washington Carver discovered 300 different uses for a mere peanut. Again, a simple thought magnified by a thousand.

- Your first single-minded effort may be to find your purpose.

- You will gain greater respect for your purpose when you fully understand it is the vehicle to obtain every desire of your heart.

- Single-mindedness is attained through total cooperation of the heart, mind and body. When those three units operate in unison toward one objective, the result is success.

- Success is scary because not only must you do all you can to reach the top, but also to make it to the highest level, *you must abandon your fears and jump!*

STAGE 9
BUILDING YOUR EMPIRE

Brick By Brick

– STAGE NINE –

"We cannot seek or attain health, wealth, learning, justice or kindness in general. Action is always specific, concrete, individualized, unique."

Benjamin Jowett

ACTION!

Manipulating Matter Into Form

All other tenets in this book are meaningless without this key principle – action is the motivating force in the universe that produces all results. Thought absent of action is a dream.

Contrary to popular belief, you cannot "think and grow rich." Although the thinking aspect is relevant to creating the proper mindset for attracting riches, it cannot, in and of itself, produce its monetary equivalent.

Those thoughts you think, those visions dancing in your head can only reach fruition through action. And, the action that produces results must be direct. Life does not respond to what you think, what you hope or what you desire. Life only responds to precisely directed action.

If thought is the mother of invention, then action is its midwife. For it is through action that matter is manipulated into form. Every great thought that made its way from the imagination realm to the physical canvas was escorted by action.

Expanding You

"The mind, once expanded to the dimensions of larger ideas, never returns to its original size," said Oliver Wendell Holmes. He was right, but unfortunately most people never take advantage of his knowledge.

Many people live their entire lives in the city of their birth, thinking the same thoughts and doing the same things. If you did move away and ever wanted to go back in time, all you have to do is visit your hometown. People who stay at the same conscious level, day in and day out, never grow – and the sad fact is they don't even recognize they are not growing.

Those individuals at the top are not necessarily the best on the planet, but they had the audacity to step out on their dream and take action. Every major city has a "playground legend" who didn't make it to the NBA. He had the talent, but he didn't follow through to victory. He settled for being the one who "could" have made it.

You've probably heard the saying, "Reach for the moon. Even if you miss, you will land among the stars." A valuable secret is hidden in that phrase. Your ability to discover who you are and what you are capable of can only come as a result of placing yourself in situations that are greater than you have ever experienced.

In other words, when you reach for a level higher than you have ever been (*the moon*), you stretch yourself and discover talents within yourself that at least place you where you belong (*among the stars*).

Begin today identifying opportunities that stretch you. Place yourself in settings where you can meet new people. Don't wait for them to come to you. Go to them. Introduce yourself, tell a joke, shake hands, and make eye contact.

This is your time on the planet. Be bold and audacious as you make your way. Let action be your ruling star, and life will bend to your resolve. Move forward through your fear, understanding you are its master, and when you tell it to recede, it must obey. Theodore Roosevelt put it this way:

"It is not the critic who counts, not the man who points out how the strong man stumbled, or where the doer of deeds could have done better. The credit belongs to the man who is actually in the arena, whose face is marred by dust and sweat and blood, who strives valiantly, who errs and comes short again and again, who knows the great enthusiasms, the great devotions, and spends himself in a worthy cause, who at best knows achievement and who at the worst if he fails at least fails while daring greatly so that his place shall never be with those cold and timid souls who know neither victory nor defeat."

Action – The Destiny-Maker

It's been said, "Action equals habit, habit equals character, and character equals destiny." In other words, "Action leads to destiny." The totality of your destiny is hidden from you right now. You may have a feeling about who you are and what you want to be, but the extent of your greatness is unknown.

Life speaks to each of us through urges and circumstances. What you may consider the worst time of your life may be life's way of pushing you to the change you have to make. You may experience a time where everything in your life is going haywire. As a result, you may change jobs, relationships or cities. Only after you make the change do you recognize you ended up where you needed to be.

Be on the constant lookout for urges that signal a time for change. Those life-urgings may be telling you it's time to act or move in a new direction. Your actions at that time will allow you to catch your proverbial bus – or miss it!

Action Creates Energy

Just like a good workout leaves you feeling vibrant and ready to tackle the world, action produces energy that allows you to increase your efforts. The concept is simple – the more you lift, the more you want to lift. The farther you run, the farther you want to run.

The best way to generate energy is through action. You may think you do not have the energy for a workout, but if you put your gym clothes on, you may find you have the desire to exercise. The action of putting on your workout gear triggers a workout mindset and produces the energy to get it done.

When faced with a project you don't have the energy for, help yourself by doing the action required by the project. Every project looks bigger when viewed through your eyes. Action is its equalizer and your liberator.

Action – The Fear Conqueror

Noted author James Allen said, *"Doubt and fear are the great enemies of knowledge, he who does not slay them – thwarts himself at every step."* You cannot bring the fullness of your talents to the surface if your thoughts are shrouded with fear.

The action of identifying and facing the things you fear allows you to control the outcome. For instance, if you are afraid of snakes, visit a place where snakes are handled in a controlled environment. After a while, you will become used to the snake's movement. The more knowledge you gain about snakes, the easier it will be to overcome your fear of them.

Every person at the height of his game has identified, challenged and conquered his fears. When you observe great actors, golfers, boxers, lawyers, doctors, etc., you will recognize they appear fearless.

Those individuals are human, and they do experience fear. The difference is they learned how to react when their fear buttons are triggered. Through identification of the fear and by placing themselves in situations where that fear is produced, they taught themselves how to control the impulse.

Those individuals challenged their fears. They applied the necessary action to put themselves in control and not let fear control them. Every fear falls to direct action. There is nothing on this planet greater than you. You have been granted dominion over this world and everything in it. The application of action allows you to conquer your fears and become the great person you were intended to be.

"You are never given a dream without also being given the power to make it true."

Richard Bach

– STAGE NINE –
WORTH REMEMBERING

- Action is the motivating force in the universe that produces all results. Thought absent of action is a dream.

- Contrary to popular belief, you cannot "think and grow rich." Although the thinking aspect is relevant to creating the proper mindset for attracting riches, it cannot, in and of itself, produce its monetary equivalent.

- Life does not respond to what you think, what you hope or what you desire. Life only responds to precisely directed action.

- If thought is the mother of invention, then action is its midwife.

- Every complex act can be simplified through repetitive action.

- The best way to generate energy is through action.

- When you stand still and only imagine what you can or cannot do, you stifle your growth and impede your progress.

- When faced with fear, most people capitulate, give up and abandon their dreams.

- Every person at the height of his game has identified, challenged and conquered his fears.

- Action allows you to conquer your fears and become the great person you were intended to be.

STAGE 10
DOING WHAT
OTHERS WON'T DO

Having What Others Won't Have

– STAGE TEN –

"A good name is rather to be chosen
than great riches."

Proverbs 22:1

NAME POWER!

Your Most Valuable Tool

Your name is the single most powerful tool you possess as it relates to your personal value. You are your name. How a person responds to hearing your name reflects how he will respond to you.

As the Bible states, *"A good name is to be chosen rather than great riches."* There are numerous examples of individuals who have stifled their ability to generate wealth due to a bad name. O.J. Simpson became one of the most hated men on the planet after he was on trial for murder. O.J. was beloved by millions (you can still picture the image of him running through the airport in the Hertz commercials). In one stroke he went from hero to zero.

Famed entertainer Michael Jackson was a household darling. He dominated the 1980s and 1990s with his flashy style of dance and performing. Charges of child molestation, coupled with his curious (putting it lightly) behaviors caused tremendous damage to his image and name. A story is told of a young man who actually had his name changed from Michael Jackson because he no longer could take the joking he received.

Your name will stay with you the rest of your life (unless you legally change it). Your name travels to places that you are unaware of – for instance, a group of people can be involved in a conversation, and your name may come up. Those people may not know you personally but will have an entire conversation about you based on what they have heard about you (or your name).

Whatever perception your name carries will dictate the attitude in which you are discussed. A good name will gain you positive ground in the conversation; a bad name will increase your infamy. Individuals believe and act on perception (not reality). Do all that is within your power to maintain the perception of good when it comes to your name.

A good name can at least place you in the running for a power position or great opportunity. A bad name can disqualify you before the selection process even begins. That is a valuable lesson for anyone seeking to climb the ladder of success and distinguish himself among the players.

Some people easily acquire name power. A family member may have reached celebrity status, thus anyone wearing the last name reaped the rewards. That does not necessarily mean a free pass through life. You probably can recall instances when a sibling, spouse, son or daughter – through negative behavior – brought disgrace to a powerful family name.

Building Name Power

There are many ways to build name power. The easiest often is the most overlooked. Living a decent life is the No. 1 way to establish your name in any market. Attributes such as honest, God-loving, respectful and good-hearted go a long way in the development of a good name.

To add power to your name, you have to do powerful things. You cannot gain power without risk. The greater the power you seek, the greater the risk you must be prepared to undertake. You must be willing to expose yourself to failure if you are to reap the reward of "Name Power!"

Actor Brad Pitt played the role of Achilles in the 2004 movie *Troy*. Achilles was the most feared warrior in all the land. He fought and won many battles, and his name was highly revered. One day the king challenged an opposing king to battle using their armies. The opposing king countered, offering his best warrior against the king's best. The king agreed and summoned Achilles.

A young messenger boy was sent to find Achilles and tell him the king needed him. When the young boy arrived at Achilles' tent, he found him asleep. After waking Achilles and waiting while he dressed, the young boy said, *"The man you are fighting is the biggest man I have ever seen. I wouldn't want to fight him."* Achilles looked down upon the child and said, *"That is why no one will remember your name."*

Employee Name Power

If you are seeking a promotion, you can gain name power by being the best employee at your current job. By doing so, you will gain a good name with your boss who will in turn speak highly of you when it's time for your advancement. Seek to exceed expectations in your current capacity, and watch your reputation grow.

If you have damaged your name in your current capacity, there are ways to restore it. The first rule you must understand is, "You cannot fix a problem at the same conscious level it was created."

That means if a problem was created by words, it cannot be solved by words alone. The problem created by words can only be effectively resolved by consistent action. We are aware that words represent 7% of how people "hear" us. For that reason, restoring a bad name requires a commitment to excellence.

To restore a bad name you must incrementally exceed expectation. The key word here is incrementally. Do not try to gain the acceptance of those you wish to impress overnight. Plot your course, and plan your strategy step by step.

Your first effort will be to understand what went wrong and how you gained a negative reputation. You may want to call a meeting with your supervisor and gain insight as to how you are perceived. That is difficult for most people because it opens them up for criticism. Accepting criticism is a requisite for growth.

Next, identify areas where you can make immediate changes. For instance, arriving to work early, volunteering for an extra assignment or helping the team with a project. You will experience resistance initially, so keep your objective solidly in your mind, and you will overcome the obstacles.

After a while, people will begin to recognize your "new" approach. Your consistent efforts will signal a "real" change in you. You will notice individuals speaking to you who heretofore would never take the time. As you continue producing positive actions, you will gain the positive name power you deserve.

The aforementioned scenario is interchangeable with other scenarios in your life. It can be used with marriages, relationships and any situation that involves conflict. Keep in mind, *a problem cannot be remedied at the same conscious level it was created.* The way to overcome a negative image is through consistent positive actions.

Career Name Power

If you are on a career path and wish to gain name power, you can do so through self-mastery and "power association." Self-mastery is the art of refining your skills and talents to the point of mastery. Power association is connecting with people of influence in a way that benefits your end objective.

First, put yourself through an exhaustive disciplined regimen that produces excellence in your field. The key word is "excellence." You must identify the bar and reach for the highest level in your field. You do so by tenaciously challenging yourself to produce superior results.

Once you reach a level of excellence, you can enlist a mentor from the greats in your field. Many people who make it to the top don't mind taking a young starling under their wings. And, connecting with an influential mentor will increase your name power.

The best way to attract a big name is simply to ask. Don't be a wimp. Reach out and ask a potential mentor for assistance. As long as you are not asking for money, you will be surprised at how effective the process is.

To start, write a letter expressing your appreciation of that person's commitment to excellence. Please do yourself a favor and research the person and his accomplishments before you write. (Never call first.)

Never underestimate the power of ego-stroking. Powerful people have committed countless hours to becoming who they are and don't mind someone recognizing their sacrifice. Take the time and let them know you have done your homework. Acknowledge their accomplishments, and watch them open up to you.

Entrepreneur Name Power

As an entrepreneur, your job of garnering name power can be difficult. You are surrounded by businesses that may have deeper pockets than yours, thus making you a small fish in a big pond. Being highly creative, fearless and customer-focused are attributes that allow you to swim with the big fish and earn their respect.

As an entrepreneur, you first must establish your product. It doesn't matter whether it's chicken dinners or professional speaking – the first art you must master is "product separation."

Product separation occurs when your product out-distances similar products in your market. That means when people think of purchasing a particular item or service and they have many options, they instinctively choose yours.

Many would-be entrepreneurs fall into the trap of selling items "they" like. A concert promoter, for instance, brought a band to town he thought was great. When few people showed up for the show, he was distraught. He never took the time to research his target audience to ascertain their likes and dislikes. He didn't do his homework and paid the price – literally.

As an entrepreneur, your name power and product name power are synonymous. Seek ways to get your name in every publication possible. Open your mind to smaller publications, and discover ways in which your product and successes can be considered "newsworthy."

The more often people see your company name, the greater "name recognition" for you. Then the next time they need your particular service, they may call you. If you can pass the "product quality test," you will gain new customers.

What's in a Name?

What's in a name? Everything! A name carries psychological power that goes beyond the name itself. People naturally associate power and credibility to certain names. Nike, Coke, Bill Gates and Tiger Woods are a few names people recognize around the world.

People buy names. Whether they're buying clothing, food, cars or people, the established name stands a better chance of getting the nod. Therefore, it is imperative that you are cognizant of your name and what you are – or are not – doing to make it special.

*By power of a name, doors open,
stature adorned, and advantage is gained.*

We Shall 217

– STAGE TEN –
WORTH REMEMBERING

- Your name is the single most powerful tool you possess as it relates to your personal value.

- How a person responds to hearing your name reflects how he will respond to you.

- A good name can at least place you in the running for a power position or great opportunity. A bad name can disqualify you before the selection process even begins.

- To add power to your name, you have to do powerful things. You cannot gain power without risk.

- The greater the power you seek, the greater the risk you must be prepared to undertake.

- If you have damaged your name in your current capacity, there are ways to restore it. The first rule you must understand is, *"You cannot fix a problem at the same conscious level it was created."*

- Self-mastery is the art of refining your skills and talents to the point of mastery. Power association is connecting with people of influence in a way that benefits your end objective.

- After waking Achilles and waiting while he dressed, the young boy said, *"The man you are fighting is the biggest man I have ever seen. I wouldn't want to fight him."* Achilles looked down upon the child and said, *"That is why no one will remember your name."*

STAGE 11
THE FINISH LINE

Job Well Done!

– STAGE ELEVEN –

*"I'm going to make you rich, Bud Foxx –
rich enough where you don't have to waste time."*

**Actor Michael Douglas in the
1987 movie Wall Street**

FREEDOM!

The Finish Line

The person who works for no one is the freest among us. That rare human being wakes up in the morning when his eyes open, not when the alarm clock goes off. He travels the country and stays in the finest hotels, paid for by others' money, not his own.

His days belong to him. He is free to do whatever he does best. He sits in his personal music studio or in front of his computer typing pages of his next book. Or maybe he "painfully" plays a round of golf at one of the most famous golf courses in the world, preparing for his next million-dollar tournament.

It's not luck or a silver spoon that produced his fate – it was tenacity, commitment and purpose. Struggle, pain, failure and disappointment forged him into mental granite and created something mere mortals worship. While others stopped and submitted to life's vicious assault, this warrior faced himself, looked hard at who he was and determined for him there was more.

When you tenaciously strive to build yourself into a marketable product, you become just that – marketable. Your efforts will allow you to call your own shots and live a life of freedom.

Microsoft owner Bill Gates, stock guru Warren Buffet and media icon Oprah Winfrey all worked tenaciously to be giants in their industries. Therefore, they play by their own rules. Their days belong to them, and no one stands over their shoulders and dictates their moves. They don't allow anyone to scold them because they missed a meeting or didn't perform up to snuff.

When you decide to stop working eight hours a day, and choose to work 16 to 20 hours, you will be on your way to earning the right to live a free life. That type of commitment must yield a return, and the benefits to you are enormous.

Most people, however, choose the opposite approach. They think they are playing it safe by working for someone else and taking home a paycheck. They are paid for eight hours of work, but really work about five hours (minus talking to co-workers and slacking off).

If you want to continue receiving less than who you are, you can follow that path. However, if you want to maximize your life, you will begin to do what's necessary to gain ownership of your destiny.

The Playing Field

In today's job market, there is no such thing as "workplace security." In the past, an employee spent his entire career at one company. Those days are long gone. The reality of business these days revolves around mergers, takeovers and downsizing. Factor in foreign labor at reduced cost, and the landscape gets pretty murky.

In the past, one person was responsible for doing one job. In today's workplace, one person is responsible for two or three jobs with no increase in pay. The demands outweigh the return, but with no options in sight, what can an employee do? High demands, absent of control, equal stress.

401K and Social Security

An interesting dynamic of the human equation is people generally don't think about old age in tangible terms. The average 21-year-old, for instance, thinks in immortal terms. Most young adults are so caught up with life and its many twists and turns that getting old never crosses their minds in a "real sense."

On the other hand, some individuals rely on their 401K plans to take care of them when they retire. They figure since they worked for 20 years, they are entitled to relax because their 401K plans will take care of them the rest of their lives.

That faulty belief leads to much disillusionment and frustration. Unfortunately, many wake up to the reality they never will be able to truly retire. And often the awakening occurs too late to change their circumstances.

Here's a simple way to view your retirement in monetary terms. If you amassed $240,000 in your 401K plan over the course of your career and lived 20 years beyond your retirement, you would have only $1,000 a month to live on for those 20 years. In other words, you would have successfully worked your way into living below the poverty line.

If you don't believe me, do the math:
$1,000 a month x 12 months = $12,000
$12,000 x 10 years = $120,000
$120,000 x 2 (representing two 10-year periods) = $240,000

The battle for Social Security dollars continues, and who knows where it will end? Every White House administration views that large pot of taxpayers' dollars with leprechaun eyes and attempts to claim it. At times when the administration over-spends and needs to bail itself out, it concocts ways to shift the use of those dollars. By the time you or I retire, there may not be a viable Social Security plan available to us.

Never Waste Time

When you polish your talent, mind, spirit and body to the point you become one with your purpose, your value will be unimaginable. As a result of your studies and self-investment, your confidence will increase measurably. And, people you do business with will experience your power, too.

Constant study in your field leads to proficiency and discovery. Through your intense search of information, you will learn to forecast future developments and hypothesize previous theories.

Soon others will hear about your efforts and invite you to expound on your views. Your circle of influence will begin to expand, and new doors will open for you. You will become one with your calling and stand solid on your knowledge.

The time will come for you to step out on your own and present your thoughts, products or services to the world. Your prior accomplishments will act as your resume, and your entry into the marketplace will be unchallenged.

Time is a valuable commodity, and when you are a decision-maker, your time is money. As a decision-maker, you may find you no longer stand in line to catch an airplane. Instead, you walk out to your private jet. Or, rather than waiting in the lobby for a business meeting, you are ushered right in to the executive suite. Your self-mastery finally will pay off, and you no longer have to waste time.

Free is the person who controls each day and is unbridled in his quest for life. Albert Einstein said, *"Everything that is really great and awe-inspiring is created by the individual who can labor in freedom."*

In the words of the Greek historian and author Thucydides, *"The secret of happiness is freedom, and the secret to freedom is courage. The bravest are surely those who have the clearest vision of what is before them, glory and danger alike, and yet notwithstanding, go out to meet it."*

He who attempts to live in freedom by doing nothing while his legs are yet strong will find himself wanting when his autumn days arrive. He will discover to his discomfort that what he considered freedom actually was the prison from which pain and suffering become his tormenting companions.

End each day by asking, *"What did I do today to make my dream of tomorrow come true?"* When you can answer that question with confidence and exceed your own expectations, you will live a life of passion, and the freedom you always dreamed of will be yours.

From spirit – to flesh – to spirit,
We are in this world for a minute.
Learn well the lessons of this day,
Perfectly crafted so you may
Be better, yea, never the same,
Than that brilliant day you came.

We Shall 217

– STAGE ELEVEN –
WORTH REMEMBERING

- When you tenaciously strive to build yourself into a marketable product, you become just that – marketable.

- Microsoft owner Bill Gates, stock guru Warren Buffet and media icon Oprah Winfrey all tenaciously worked to be giants in their industries.

- They play by their own rules.

- Their days belong to them, and no one stands over their shoulders and dictates their moves.

- When you decide to stop working eight hours a day, and choose to work 16 to 20 hours, you will be on your way to earning the right to live a free life.

- In today's job market, there is no such thing as "workplace security."

- The reality of business these days revolves around mergers, takeovers and downsizing. Factor in foreign labor at reduced cost, and the landscape gets pretty murky.

- High demands, absent of control, equal stress.

- You can change course and begin doing what you need to liberate your life and gain the control you desire.

- Constant mining of your internal diamond field will produce unimaginable treasures – "You Are The Money!"

STAGE 12
GIVING BACK –
SERVING OTHERS

Leaving A Legacy

– STAGE TWELVE –

Restrict not you mind by sifting only through the finite, but allow your mind to bring forth treasures from the realm of the infinite.

We Shall 217

GETTING CONNECTED

Finding Your Anchor

History is replete with men and women who used unscrupulous means to acquire wealth. The financial landscape is littered with the names of those individuals and the infamy of their quests. The empty pursuit of wealth, absent of some humanitarian gain, is equivalent to obtaining sex without love.

If the obtainment of wealth is your objective, you may reach the finish line fraught with disillusionment. The wise person understands it is not what an individual takes from the planet that makes him eternally rich, it is what he gives back that ultimately makes him wealthy.

The beauty of this world cannot be purchased with paper money. Those tenets that make our earthly stay enjoyable come from a giving spirit and a wealthy soul. To fully understand that assertion, one only needs to read about lottery winners who won a million+ dollars and then lost everything.

A Non-Recurring Miracle

Do you know who you are? Do you know the great heights you are capable of reaching? It is time to come to terms with the enormity of your powers. You can only create at your maximum potential when you understand who you are potentially.

Just look at a trained elephant, and you will see your own experience. The elephant is one of the largest and strongest creatures on the planet. Yet through training, this large creature is conditioned to believe it can't even break a rope tied to its leg.

The elephant believes that so much it *doesn't even try*. At birth shackled by a huge chain, the young elephant could not break free no matter how hard it tried. By the time it grew into a full-grown elephant, the trainer no longer needed to place a chain around its leg. All that was needed was a rope.

The *process* accomplished what it was intended to do – make a creature that was capable of performing tremendous feats with its strength *believe* it could only operate at a fragment of its potential.

The trained elephant scenario holds multiple learning examples that are transferable to our own experience. One interesting dynamic is the time frame in which the elephant views the rope as a chain. The conditioning process experienced by the elephant is designed to last a lifetime. You can visit the circus 10 years later, and the elephant's condition will not have changed. Ten years later, it still views the rope as a chain.

The human mind is wired much the same way, as it relates to input and stimuli. Once a person accepts a certain pattern of behavior and plays it out over a course of time, it becomes a habit. That habit played out becomes reality. And the acceptance of that reality will lead him to his destiny. As Newton's first law states, *"An object at rest tends to stay at rest and an object in motion tends to stay in motion with the same speed and in the same direction unless acted upon by an unbalanced force."*

Think about what would happen if the elephant awakened to its real self. Can you imagine its state of confusion? Its first question probably would be, "Who am I?" Its second and more probing question, "What am I truly capable of accomplishing?"

You, too, have underestimated your true power. The reason is nobody told you who you are in a way you can understand and apply. It's time for you to come face-to-face with the "*real you.*" Are you ready to break the rope?

In your hand you wear an ancient symbol. On Earth, we call it a fingerprint. That secret symbol is equivalent to a Social Security number. (Each connects you to its maker.) The U.S. government gave you a Social Security number; the Creator gave you a fingerprint.

Your Social Security number is yours alone. No other human on this planet has it. The same is true of your fingerprint. Your Social Security card connects you with every other citizen of the United States; your fingerprint connects you to the universe.

How can you measure the truth of that assertion? Answer this question, "What abilities do we attribute to God?" Answer: He has the ability to create something from nothing. He can speak things into existence. He is *The First and Last, The One and Only.*

Now let's take a look at the gifts you possess. Can you create something from nothing? Yes, you can. Picture the world before there were buildings. Now see the world as it currently exists. Where there was nothing, we have created something.

Let's go further into the equation. Can you speak things into existence? Yes, you can. Remember the mountain climbers in Chapter 3? (The three who said, "I will.") They spoke their victory into existence, and the mind, body and spirit obeyed their command.

Lastly, how many people on this planet are exactly like you? How many people who have ever been on this planet were exactly like you? And how many people, when you are gone, will come to this planet and be exactly like you?

If you said "none," you are right. I guess that makes you "the first, the last, beginning and ending, the one and only you." And how does the Father describe Himself? – *The Alpha and Omega, The Beginning and The Ending, The First and The Last* (Revelations 22:13).

He left you a symbol – a physical way to identify your connection to him. You've been searching for the connection – now your search is over.

God's Omnipresence

Over the course of time, man has sought to answer the question of God's "Omnipresence." It was beyond man's comprehension how God could be everywhere at the same time. The answer escapes us because we view the Creator in human terms and through human lenses. We consider the physical aspect of being everywhere at the same time and measure the possibilities through finite processes.

The fact that we view things in "disconnected terms" – such as the sun being separate from the moon and the Earth being separate from humans – keeps us from seeing the total picture. When you attempt to see things as connected and parts of a whole, a different picture emerges.

Let me give you a basic example of connectedness and omnipresence. In most large corporations with personal computers, there is the main computer referred to as the "mainframe." The mainframe is the source of all information. All the other computers in the building are plugged into or connected to the mainframe. Try to view the mainframe as the universe, and try to see you and me as the computers.

Even though each computer operates independently, its source of information comes from being connected to the mainframe. The mainframe is aware of every piece of information all computers are using – *all at the same time.*

Some computers can access an even greater amount of information because they know the secret password (or in spiritual terms, they possess a gift). The password allows them to access information stored at deeper levels in the mainframe.

Connecting to the Mainframe

You, too, are connected to the greatest information source in the universe – not separate but connected. The art you must master is experiencing your connectedness. So how do you do that?

The first step, of course, is *"knowing."* You must know you are not a mere speck of dust dwarfed by the great universe, but you are part of the universe itself. It produced you, and your very uniqueness is a testament to that relationship.

When you apply "knowing" to that revelation, you begin to experience a feeling of being overwhelmed. You begin to actually feel the power surge running through you and all around you. To complete this experience, you must consciously connect yourself mentally and spiritually with the source of all information.

The keyword is *consciously.* There must be a conscious effort. Close your eyes, and consciously accept who you are – not the helpless, fear-filled person we all feel like at times, but the glorious miracle that is you.

Keep in mind, you do not need to see an event right now to acknowledge your connection. Feel comfortable with knowing the information you are seeking is in fact seeking you, and your need to experience connectedness will be met and satisfied by the living force itself.

There is no need to force anything. That is what makes the experience so gratifying – the knowing, the discovery and ultimately the confirmation of who you really are. You begin to be like a great painter or artist experiencing the ebb and flow of the universe itself. When you begin to connect at that level, you no longer look to external results to assure you are on the right course.

You become fully aware that once a great idea enters your consciousness, it is a reality at that time. It is as *fixed* and *concrete* as the city you were traveling to in Chapter 3. Your task is to find the connectors that will bring that great idea out onto this earthly plane of existence. The idea and all facets of the idea are available intact somewhere in the mainframe.

Understand this – write it down somewhere, everywhere. It is impossible to picture in its entirety an idea that cannot be produced. The mind is funny. Once it hears a statement like that, it immediately begins to think of something that can't possibly be done.

Keep in mind, remote controls, hand-held lighters, satellites, rockets, submarines and many other major inventions were thought to be impossible. If you can conceive it, you can achieve it. Sound familiar? It's truer than you know.

The universe always gives us examples of truth in tangible expressions. You can relate to the invisible connection of things by recognizing how a single song can be popular across the planet. What is that familiar chord that transcends cultures and gender and causes everyone who hears certain tones to vibrate with the same feeling? It's our connectedness.

The Download Process

Let me give you a final example of connecting to information and downloading it into your consciousness. Do you believe when you watch television, the actors and actresses are actually in the television set? Of course not! The particles of information are floating around in the air. When you turn on your television, an antenna goes up and allows the particles of information to be downloaded into your television set.

That means even though your television is off, the information is still out there. Take a moment and contrast that thought with "universal information." If you allow yourself to "conceive" of information being available to you on a "universal" plane, you have an opportunity to learn how to use your internal antenna.

Your possession of an internal antenna has been well documented. Although most of us never refer to it as an antenna, it functions at the same level. Our intuition is a "surface-level" antenna; it is the mechanism we use to "feel" things we cannot see.

You probably can recall a time when you simply knew something and did not know how you knew it. That is the working of your internal antenna. What you must learn to do is trust your inner-system.

The stronger your antenna, the more information you are able to download. The more connected you are, the stronger your antenna. For many people, the Bible, the Koran or their instrument of worship strengthens their antenna. The Bible, Koran or that instrument of worship acts as an encoded message that once digested allows for pure information from the universe to be interpreted.

When you begin to function at that level of understanding, you walk in accordance with your true mission. You no longer allow doubt to rob you of what your intuition is telling you. You move forward with the knowledge you are on the right path.

Opportunities begin to come your way that line up with your expectations, and you vibrate with greater intensity. You begin to feel connected to your vision and act on your impulses. People show up from out of the blue to assist you in matters that are in keeping with your mission.

Connectedness and Wealth Creation

The greatest accomplishment any human can realize in life is "serving others." As you learn to attract wealth into your world, be mindful of its true purpose. It's not how many cars you can buy or how many houses you can purchase with your wealth that will make you a success. It is what you give back to the planet that will allow the universe to acknowledge, *"A job well done."*

Sincere ambitions endear you to others and allow you to gain entry into powerful places. People at the top have to trust you. They must be able to look you in your eyes and know you have high integrity and a sound character.

Character is what you do when no one is watching. Integrity is doing what you said you would do when you said you would do it. The higher you advance, the more power you will assume. And as the Bible states, *"To whoever much is given, of him will much be required."* (St. Luke 12:48)

You must seek to "show yourself approved" in all things you do in life. You do that by taking the high ground, even when others seek to pull you astray. In the end, you will live a life that testifies of goodness, and the Father will grant you the desires of your heart.

In one man's mind, God plants the seed
of tomorrow that it should grow
and carry the world into it.

We Shall 217

– STAGE TWELVE –
WORTH REMEMBERING

- History is replete with men and women who used unscrupulous means to acquire wealth.

- The empty pursuit of wealth, absent of some humanitarian gain, is equivalent to obtaining sex without love.

- Do you know who you are?

- You can only create at your maximum potential when you understand what you are potentially.

- Just look at a trained elephant shackled by a mere rope, and you will see your own experience.

- You can visit the circus 10 years later, and the elephant's condition will not have changed.

- Over the course of time, man has sought to answer the question of God's "Omnipresence." It was beyond man's comprehension how God could be everywhere at the same time.

- When you attempt to see things as connected and parts of a whole, a different picture emerges.

- You must know you are not a mere speck of dust dwarfed by the great universe, but you are part of the universe itself. It produced you, and your very uniqueness is a testament to that relationship.

AFTERTHOUGHT
PUTTING IT ALL TOGETHER

The Boiled Frog Syndrome

Biologists describe a process referred to as "The Boiled Frog Syndrome." The theory states you can take a live frog and place it in a boiling pot of water, and the frog immediately will try to jump out of the water. But the outcome is much different when you take the same frog and place it in a warm pot of water and slowly turn up the heat. As the temperature rises, the frog first will begin to get groggy. As the temperature increases to a boil, the frog will allow itself to be boiled to death – without a fight.

Think about that for a moment – "The Boiled Frog Syndrome." Upon closer observation, it is interesting to note the beginning and middle process of the theory. Notice the heat must be turned up gradually so the frog doesn't even notice much difference.

You can equate this process to your early years as a child – you don't even notice the heat being applied. The heat, of course, represents demands and expectations. Being too young to understand what is taking place, you don't give it a second thought.

That aspect of the process takes place in many areas of life. An employee, for instance, may not object to a request to work an extra five minutes. The same employee may sternly object to being requested to work an additional hour. The employee can accept incremental increases that in the end add up to an hour, far easier than the latter.

Now let's take a look at the middle process. As the water begins to get hotter, the frog gets groggy. That part of the process is reflected in you giving in to the demands and expectations of your "accepted" situation.

A boss, for instance may yell at you due to his/her perception of your performance. Or, your spouse may exhibit negative behavior every time you partake in an activity he/she disagrees with. You acquiesce to the negative behavior and become robotic in your acceptance. Your system being overwhelmed gets groggy and tries to find a way to just stay out of trouble.

As we look at the final phase of the frog allowing itself to be boiled alive, an interesting position is presented. At what point does the frog give in so completely that it allows itself to be boiled? Is there no mechanism that sounds the alarm and says, "Hey, this isn't fun anymore?"

Maybe you can answer that question. If you found yourself operating in a way that literally was killing your spirit, would you jump out of it? If you discovered the way you approach making money and pursuing your dreams was never going to lead you to that end, would you stop the process?

Look around you. The *process* is easy to see. You just have to know what to watch for. Look closely into the eyes of those who have gone before you – those souls who were sold the same bill of goods as you were. You will see the lifeless expression, the frustration and the agony of a spirit who settled for less than life had to offer – a person who didn't realize the true way to wealth and happiness was discovering and capitalizing on his or her innate gifts and talents. You sadly will acknowledge the presence of a soul who gave in through negative reinforcement and became *one among many*.

A Failed Paradigm

I wrote *You Are The Money!* because I recognized how far we as the human race have moved away from living the life God intended us to live. In my humble opinion, God gave each of us the talents and gifts we need to attract wealth and abundance into our lives. I also believe those talents and gifts were intended to edify our fellow man and improve the conditions on the planet.

So what went wrong? How did we get so far from pursuing our natural talents? The answer can be summed up in one word – competition. Competition is an indigenous part of the human experience. Competition is responsible for the advancement of mankind as well as for many of the woes we experience. If you removed competition from the human equation, a different earthly picture would emerge (both pro and con).

Take a moment and picture the world without competition. Competition brings out the animal instinct in humans. Competition clouds logic to the point of non-existence in most cases. You clearly see the reality of that statement at a boxing match. People generally are appalled to see two human beings bloody each other's face, but in the name of competition the rules of engagement drastically change.

The moment money was introduced to people as a way to gain power, the competition began. The basic rules of kindness, decency and honesty gave way to the statement, "This is business (or business is war)."

When competition and money combine, you get the world as it is today. You get a world where money rules and everything else (in a vague sense of the word) becomes secondary. You get a world where people worship money and will do all manner of things to get their hands on some.

If ever the people were tricked (by whatever dark force you believe in), then surely the pursuit of money was the greatest trick ever played on human beings. That singular trick enslaved billions of people to "chasing money" and is the greatest reason millions have been sidetracked from discovering their life purpose.

What greater way could you imagine to disable humans from enjoying the life they were meant to enjoy than to cause them to abandon pursuit of their natural gifts? Pursuing money absent of talent development is equivalent to a young person choosing to sell drugs on a corner instead of going to school.

Is that to say we should not be mindful of the need for money? No. It merely says we should move to put money in its proper perspective. When we put it in perspective, we develop an understanding of what money is (a bartering tool) and what it is not (a source of worship).

Have you noticed we generally monitor critical aspects of life to see if they are working properly? Look at the environment for instance. We constantly monitor changes in climate, discuss global warming and promote recycling to do the right things to ensure our survival. Why haven't we done that with money?

Why has there been no real effort to measure the effectiveness or ineffectiveness of the pursuit of wealth? Why haven't we pushed the pause button and examined the way millions of people approach making money? If only 4.2% of the working American public makes $100,000 or more a year (according to the U.S. Senate Committee on Appropriations) while the rest struggle to make ends meet, then something is very wrong. And the fact that millions of people cannot find their way to financial freedom indicates the current wealth-generating paradigm, for most Americans, is flawed.

The Paradigm Shift

It's time for a paradigm shift. A shift is necessary when old assumptions, traditions, theories and rules fail to produce sought-after outcomes.

Try to imagine a world where individuals competed to identify and bring to surface their innate talents and gifts. Imagine how fulfilled people would be upon discovering what they do best.

Can you picture our school system as a breeding ground for personal talent? Imagine the teacher addressing the class, "Today we are going to work on discovering what each of you does best."

Now try to picture how different the world would look if everybody was functioning in accordance with their God-given talent. No longer would people experience the emptiness and frustration of working jobs that don't fulfill their inner needs. Their days would be full of excitement, working from a purpose-driven position, and the world would be the beneficiary of their efforts.

A competition where talent and gift discovery represents victory benefits the whole planet. How many people go to their graves with their talents and gifts undiscovered and unutilized? Some of the best discoveries and inventions never evolve because people pursued dollars and not the discovery of their gifts.

Since most people never were taught to look for their talents, many pursued the "acceptable" norm. Those who possessed natural, identifiable talents were encouraged to pursue occupations based on the amount of money the job paid. For example, a person who is a good talker or debater would be encouraged to pursue a law degree – yet be discouraged from a career as an advocate for the poor, even though the latter may be more in line with his or her purpose.

Although the world is full of people who possess talent compa-rable to ace golfer Tiger Woods (in other fields of endeavor), very few have an Earl Woods (Tiger's father). Earl gave Tiger something that will stay with him even after Earl is long gone. Earl gave Tiger – Tiger. In other words, Earl "drew" from Tiger, at a very young age, Tiger's pure essence and allowed him to experience his own power through victory and defeat. And in the end, Earl assisted Tiger in becoming a complete human being who would share his gift with the world.

It's time we "flip the script" to recognize the detriment of the "money competition" and begin teaching ourselves and our children the art of talent and gift identification.

JOIN THE
"I AM THE MONEY!" MOVEMENT

As founder of the *I Am the Money!* Movement, I went from chasing money (as a radio personality, concert promoter and club owner) to developing products and services to empower people and thus have attracted wealth into my world (as an author, columnist, trainer and consultant).

The difference in the life I lead now and the one I lived before my discovery is night and day. When I chased money, money was the center of my universe. I thought of ways to make money and how to get my hands on it.

My epiphany led me to write a radio training curriculum to teach teens how to strengthen their communication skills. I also wrote a speaker's training curriculum to teach speakers and others the secrets of professional speaking to enhance their personal growth and advance their careers.

I created the *You Are the Money!* series that includes this book in addition to *You Are The Money! . . . for Teens* and *You Are The Money! . . . for Kids*. The series includes an *I Am the Money!* merchandising line and an audio and video series.

My corporate consulting company provides staff development training for companies and organizations. I create Power Point presentations and workshops and train staff, management and CEOs on the effectiveness of leadership, conflict resolution, branding and team-building.

Those products and services allow me to impact the planet in a positive way and to attract wealth into my world. I make sure I exceed expectations in the delivery of my services and in turn I receive great publicity through word of mouth and testimonials, which result in repeat business. I no longer have to chase money – the money is chasing me.

I invite you to join the movement. All you have to do is denounce the old way of chasing money, start capitalizing on your innate talents and become an *I Am The Money!* warrior. When you are ready to change your life, sign on to www.totallymotivated.com and join the movement.

As an *I Am The Money!* member, you will be able to share your experiences with other like-minded people. You also can network with others who are pursuing their dreams and are on their way to living an empowered and purpose-driven life.

It's time for you to reclaim your birthright – your right to live a life of abundance and power. It's time to break free from the shackles of money-chasing and personal disempowerment. It's time to discover your purpose and bring this planet the uniqueness of you to fully understand why "You Are The Money!"

SUGGESTED READING
TOP TEN PICKS

Proverbs (A **Must-Read**, Particularly for Young Men) .....The Bible

Thick Face Black Heart ....Chin-Ning Chu

Conversations With God..................................Neale Donald Walsh

*Why Should White Guys
Have All The Fun?* ....Reginald F. Lewis &
Blair S. Walker

The Act of Will ....Roberto Assagioli

Seven Habits of Highly Effective People ....Steven Covey

The Celestine Prophecy...James Redfield

The Art of War ....Sun Tzu

Power..Robert Greene

Who Moved My Cheese?...Spencer Johnson

WORKS CITED

Allen, James, *As A Man Thinketh*. Barnes and Noble Inc., Barnes and Noble Books. 2002.

Ali, Muhammad, quoted in *When We Were Kings*. 1996 documentary.

Benioff, David, *Troy*. Warner Bros. Studios. 2004.

Edward, David and Callahan, Mike, *The Motown Story*. www.iconnect.net/home/bsnpubs/gordystory.html June 11, 1999.

Hoffman, Edward, *The Right to be Human: A Biography of Abraham Maslow*. New York: St. Martins Press. 1988.

Horowitz, David, *Robin Hood Lives*. FrontPageMagazine.com. May 24, 1997.

Kamen, Mark, Robert, *The Karate Kid*. Sony Pictures Home Entertainment. 1984.

Lucas, George, *Star Wars*. Twentieth Century Fox. 1977 & 1997.

McFarland, Marvin W. (ed.), *The Papers of Wilburand Orville Wright*. McGraw-Hill Book Co., New York pp. 1210-1214. 1953.

Nightingale, Earl, *The Strangest Secret*. BN Publishing. January 2006.

Simmel, Georg, *The Philosophy of Money*. Routledge & Kegan Paul 1978.

Wachowski, Larry and Andy, *The Matrix*. Warner Bros. Studio. March 31, 1999.

SPECIAL THANKS

SOLI DEO GLORIA
(GLORY TO GOD ALONE)

Valarie Wilson, thank you for opening the door that has led to many great opportunities. It all began with you taking a chance on me – you have my deepest gratitude. James Webb, thank you for your supportive and encouraging words.

Lynda Ireland, thank you for bringing me to New York and granting me the opportunity to "infotain" the Big Apple. You are a gracious host who knows how to put it all together.

George Fraser, thank you for teaching us all how to connect for success and why *It Takes TEAMWORK to Make the DREAM WORK.*"

Ron Williams, you really know how to put on a show! Thank you for your support. Theresa Porter, you know good talent when you see it (smile). Thank you for introducing me to Carlos. And thank you both for your hospitality while I was in Baton Rouge. Charlotte Placide, thank you for allowing me to assist you in the development of your team. You are a great leader with great vision. Continued success.

Dr. Richard Brown, thank you for believing in me. Janice Garnett, thank you for going that extra mile.

ABOUT THE AUTHOR

Wes Hall is a national motivational speaker, trainer, newspaper columnist and author. His high-impact keynote presentations have included major business conferences in New York, Phoenix, Denver and St. Louis.

He is dedicated to empowering individuals by showing them how to capitalize on their innate talents and offers training programs for corporations, business councils, school districts, youth groups and nonprofit organizations across the country. His topics focus on team-building, conflict resolution, branding and leadership.

Additionally, he shares his expertise as a top speaker and is an executive coach for professional speakers, and he has developed a curriculum for youth to improve their communication skills.

Wes got his start in the radio industry, where he worked for 25 years furthering his career at some of the top markets in the country in the Carolinas, Virginia and the San Francisco-Oakland area – the fourth largest market in America.

His career path changed after reading and listening to Les Brown, world-renowned speaker and best-selling author. Wes was professionally trained by Les Brown, and they've conducted seminars and speaking engagements together.

In 2001, Wes was named a "Successpert" by the national *Black Enterprise* magazine. He currently writes a weekly newspaper column entitled "Totally Motivated."

WHAT OTHERS ARE SAYING ABOUT
WES HALL
KEYNOTE SPEAKER/TRAINER

"You not only motivated, but moved me – moved me forward to strive for even higher heights! You engaged our audience – not a single "side" conversation was being conducted and in NY, that's truly unique. Your energy, personality and message is a must for individuals in fields that need re-charging occasionally. Thanks for being The Council's 'battery.' "

Lynda Ireland, President/CEO
New York & New Jersey Minority
Supplier Development Council

"Wes Hall was terrific! From now on we want to start off our Business Opportunity Fair with a motivational speaker like him!"
James Webb, President/CEO
St. Louis Minority Business Council

"Wes Hall left behind a successful career in radio to motivate others."
Rob Borsellino, Columnist
Des Moines Register

"Thank you for your excellent presentation. Your talk was motivating to the audience of young people and parents. The focus on establishing and directing short- and long-term goals to accomplish success both in school and in life was inspirational."
John J. Mackiel, Superintendent
Omaha Public Schools

"It is great to see such an effective motivator reaching so many different audiences. A very powerful message, reminding individuals of their unique gifts and talents, and how those gifts can benefit the world. We applaud his efforts and success in this area."
Stephanie Lederle, Executive Assistant
Get Motivated Seminars, Tampa, FL